A Global Look at the Beach Environment
and How We Use It

BEACHES IN SPACE AND TIME

Pineapple Press, Inc.
Sarasota, Florida

Dedicated to my kids and grandkids;
they all love the beach!

Inquiries should be addressed to:
Pineapple Press, Inc.
P.O. Box 3889
Sarasota, Florida 34230

www.pineapplepress.com

Library of Congress Cataloging-in-Publication Data

Davis, Richard A., Jr.
Beaches in space and time : a global look at the beach environment
and how we use it / Richard Davis. — First Edition.
pages   cm
Includes bibliographical references and index.
ISBN 978-1-56164-733-0 (pbk. : alk. paper)
1. Beaches. 2. Seashore ecology. I. Title.

GB450.2.D386 2014
551.45'7—dc23
                                                    2014020229

First Edition
10 9 8 7 6 5 4 3 2 1

Design: Doris Halle
Printed in the United States

Contents

Preface

The title of this book may bring to mind odd images of sandy beaches on Einstein's space-time continuum, but if you think like a geologist, space just means somewhere on our planet and time means, well, that ordinary progression most people think it means. But time in the geological sense can mean a very long progression measured in millions of years.

The beach is one of the most visited places on the planet. Some folks go to the same one over and over for recreation. Others may be more curious and visit many different beaches. Those who are very committed to the beach often choose to live on it or very near it. Some will have a second home at the beach for frequent visits.

Beaches exist everywhere on earth from the Arctic to the Antarctic all around the globe. We normally think of the beach as a place where water meets the land with sand. That is certainly true for most beaches, but there are wide variations in kinds of beaches. Some beaches are muddy, some strewn with boulders; some are wide and flat, others narrow and steep. The other aspect of the beach environment that is present everywhere is the presence of waves. There is great variation in waves in both space and time. The location of a beach pretty much dictates the wave climate. Weather is a major factor in many ways. The orientation of the shoreline relative to the approach of the waves is also important. The geology of the coast adjacent to the beach, both its composition and its size, is also a factor in the nature of the beach.

This book is designed for the person who is fond of the beach and wants to learn about its character, how it functions, its variety around the globe, and how and why it is visited by so many folks for so many reasons. The many color photos illustrate and enhance the text to make the science of the beach more real to the reader. A glossary of terms is also provided.

Keep in mind that beaches change continuously and that major changes can occur in a single day during a storm. For those reasons there are photographs in the book that were taken some years ago that will show a beach that looks different at this time.

You will note that many of the photos are credited to various sources and people. Their generosity in making them available for inclusion is greatly appreciated. Several of the diagrams have been produced or modified by Fabio Moretzshon.The Harte Research Institute for the Gulf of Mexico at Texas A&M University–Corpus Christi provided a variety of support for the production of the manuscript.

1 Beach Processes

INTRODUCTION

Scientists have determined that the earth is 4.6 billion years old. It began as a huge dust cloud of diverse gases that consolidated through the action of gravity, forming a mass that evolved into the earth. The *lithosphere,* hydrosphere, and atmosphere evolved, and a semblance of an equilibrium system among these three systems developed. The lithosphere had a largely volcanic source that eventually became the three main layers of the crust, mantle, and core. Included in the crust are igneous, sedimentary, and metamorphic rocks. Volcanic activities were widespread, expelling water vapor that eventually produced the hydrosphere. Most of the hydrosphere rested on the lithosphere and included the oceans, lakes, and streams. There was also groundwater beneath the surface of the lithosphere. The uppermost layer is the atmosphere, primarily composed of nitrogen and hydrogen as well as other gases. Oxygen came somewhat later as volcanic activity proceeded. As the oceans evolved, they accumulated salinity from the chemical erosion of minerals and eventually established a dynamic equilibrium that maintains the salinity concentration as we know it today.

These conditions provided the basis for our present surface environments, both on the land and in the sea. Many of these can be seen in a diagram of the hydrologic cycle (figure 1.1). The *beach* is simply a very narrow environment composed of sediment and that separates land from water. It can be present at the edge of lakes, seas, oceans, and even on riverbanks. Weather has always varied over the surface of the earth, but it has common patterns in this cycle regardless of location. Atmospheric moisture forms into clouds that, when saturated, lead to precipitation. This phenomenon is the fundamental process on the earth surface that produces erosion and deposition. The rain leads to the development of streams, and this flowing water can contribute to both physical and chemical

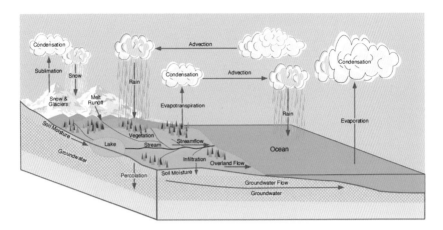

Figure 1.1
Hydrologic cycle showing the main elements of the earth's surface

erosion. Streams also deposit sediment as sand bodies in the channels and as widespread mud deposits on the flood plains. The streams may feed lakes that form in small to large enclosed basins on the land surface, or they may empty into the ocean. Rain also penetrates into the lithosphere to become part of the groundwater.

The earth's surface includes mountains and plains with coasts and ocean basins. Streams carry erosion-produced sediment to their mouths, where it can be deposited as *deltas* or moved along the coast as beaches. A beach is simply unconsolidated sediment along the shoreline regardless of composition or particle size. The sediment may reach the shoreline via transport by streams, it also might be eroded directly from the rocks in cliffs or bluffs along the shoreline, or it might be reworked by *waves* and currents from older sediment in the shallow water near the shoreline. Most characteristics of the beach have been fairly typical since "the beginning of time," but some things have changed. The changes have been produced by the evolution of various plants and animals, especially humans. We know that humans can alter their environment, and the beach is certainly included.

Understanding beaches through time and space means understanding what a beach is and how it works through geologic time and throughout the globe. In the human era the beach has played important roles in war, economics, sports, art, and other arenas.

NATURE OF THE BEACH

In order to understand how a beach works it is necessary to consider the processes to which it is subjected. The beach environment is at the contact point between all three of the main earth systems: the hydrosphere, atmosphere, and lithosphere. The range in the motion and rate of scale of all three of these systems is great and wide-ranging. The scales of change in the beach may be as short as a single wave during a storm or as long as millennia when sea level is changing.

PROCESSES

The starting point for beach processes is the weather. Large patterns of weather form latitudinal belts around the globe, for example, the westerlies and the easterlies. These weather patterns are continuous and are related to the rotation of the earth and the latitude at which they occur. There are seasonal variations in these patterns, but overall they are predictable. Included are frontal passages, high and low pressure systems, and major storms. These events can produce processes that act directly on the beach environment.

Wind produces waves on the water surface. The friction between the moving air and the water surface causes disturbance and deformation of the otherwise flat water surface. The waves produced transport water and can physically break up rocks in the cliffs along the shoreline. Depending on how the waves approach the shoreline, they can also generate currents that will transport sediment. The size of the waves is dependent on three variables: the speed of the wind, the length of time that the wind blows over the water, and the size of the basin over which the wind is blowing. The latter is termed the *fetch*. Some large water bodies such as the Gulf of Mexico and the Mediterranean Sea are considered fetch-limited. In other words, no matter how fast the wind blows over long periods of time, the wave size is not going to achieve its potential.

Waves are the most important continuing process that influences the beach. There are small changes that occur as each wave reaches the beach. The waves move with the direction of the wind, but the water, for the most part, does not. The way that this works is that the individual water particles in a wave are moving in a circular path. The water particles in this circular path are mov-

Figure 1.2
Diagram of waves showing circular movement of water

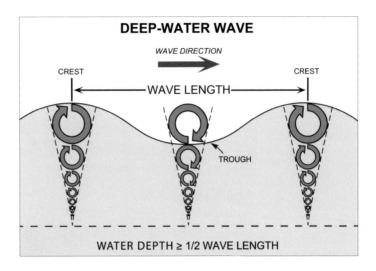

When a wave moves into shallow water, the circular water motion
beneath it begins to interact with the bottom (figure 1.3). This
ing in the direction of movement of the wave but the water itself is
not progressing forward; only the wave form moves forward. The
exception is that some of the water is moving with the wave form
due to the friction between the air and water.

The size of the circles in which the water particles are moving is
equal to the height of the wave, measured as the distance from
the bottom of the trough to the top of the crest (figure 1.2). The
length of the wave, measured from its crest to the crest of the next
wave, is also a factor in its power and ability to move sediment.
From the water surface through the water column to the seafloor,
the diameters of the circles decrease. At a depth of one-half of the
wave length, the water motion is absent. A SCUBA diver is well
aware of this water motion. Near the water surface under waves
the diver moves in a circular motion with the water particles. By
descending, it is possible for a diver to move beyond the influence
of the water motion.

When a wave moves into shallow water, the circular water motion
beneath it begins to interact with the bottom (figure 1.3). This
causes the sediment on the bottom to move. Obviously, the size
of the waves and the size of the sediment particles are factors in
the amount and rate of movement. As this phenomenon occurs,
the circular paths of the water particles become deformed into
ovals and eventually to just a back and forth motion. Eventually

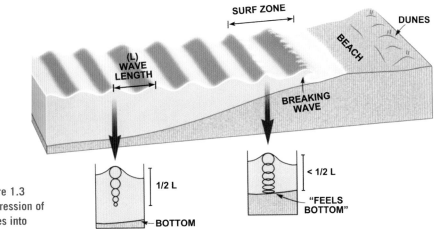

Figure 1.3 Progression of waves into shallow water and eventually to the shoreline

the top of the wave moves faster than the base due to the friction between the water and sediment on the seafloor, and the wave breaks. Breaking waves form what is called the *surf zone*.

Waves move in the direction that the wind blows. Most of the time this does not parallel the orientation of the shoreline and so the waves approach at an angle. When this happens, the circular motion within the wave interacts with the bottom and moves sediment at different positions along the wave crest. This causes the waves to bend or refract as they approach the shoreline. This *wave refraction* causes water to move in the direction of the open angle, called a *longshore current* (figure 1.4).

Figure 1.4 Wave refraction as shoreline is approached. This generates longshore currents

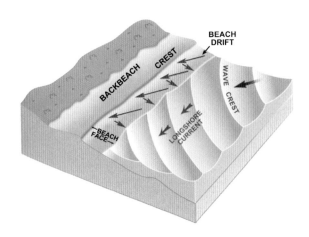

These currents can move considerable sediment under storm conditions. The waves disturb the bottom and put sediment into suspension, and then the longshore current moves the sediment along the shoreline in the surf zone where the waves break. This movement of sand along the beach is concentrated in the surf zone and has been called "the river of sand." These longshore currents can move more than a meter per second during storm conditions.

Waves break in different ways due to their size, speed, and wind conditions. There are three primary types of breaking waves; spilling, plunging, and surging (figure 1.5). *Spilling waves* are those that break under the direct influence of wind and break over some seconds, kind of like water being poured out of a glass. Spillers are generally rather short period waves—that is, it only takes a few seconds for a wave to pass a point. *Plunging waves* form from swell waves that are no longer under the direct influence of the wind. These waves curl up and crash in less than a second. They are common in longer period waves. A *surging wave* is the last breaking wave as it surges up on the beach. How a wave breaks influences what happens in terms of sand deposition and erosion on the beach.

Another important aspect of circulation associated with the beach environment is the rip current system. *Rip currents* are produced by the interaction of wave and wave-generated currents with the *longshore sandbars* that parallel the beach in the surf zone. Some water is transported landward as the waves move to the beach. This produces what is called *setup,* a temporary accumulation of water at the shore that is returned seaward via gravity. Typically this setup returns through low places, called saddles, in the longshore sandbars (figure 1.6). These currents are not important sediment transporters but they are hazards to swimmers. It is common for swimmers to be carried seaward unless they swim parallel to the shore. Rip currents are narrow and a few strokes can be the difference between significant danger and safety.

Setup can also contribute to another type of circulation that is a danger to swimmers. Under high energy conditions such as during a storm when large waves and water move toward the

Figure 1.5
Different ways
in which waves
break in the
surf zone:
(a) plunging,
(b) spilling,
and (c) surging.

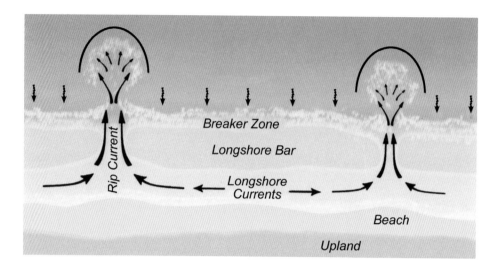

Breaker Zone

Longshore Bar

Longshore
Currents

Beach

Upland

Rip Current

**Figure 1.6
Diagram of a rip
current system**

shore, a relatively large unstable pile of water mentioned earlier, the setup, may return as *undertow*. This process is a strong seaward current just above the sea floor. Such a strong current is limited to the area just adjacent to the shoreline and can cause a person there to fall. Due to the high wave-energy conditions, that person can be unable to stand up and can be in distress.

Tides, that is, regular changes in water level, are another important influence on the beach. Astronomical tides are a result of the gravitational attraction among the sun, moon, and earth (figure 1.7). This attraction is directly proportional to the mass of the celestial bodies and inversely proportional to the square of the distance between them (Newton's Law of Universal Gravitation). This attraction causes a deformation in the envelope of water around the earth that is the oceans. As the earth rotates on its axis, the astronomical tides occur as the two bulges of this envelope move across the water surface causing the water level at the coast to rise and fall. Tides range from only a few centimeters to 15 m, depending on location. The differences are caused by the position and configuration of the shoreline. Because of the great range of tides over the earth surface, coasts have been classified as *microtidal* (<2 m), *mesotidal* (2–4 m) and *macrotidal* (>4 m). The largest tidal cycles in the world are in the Bay of Fundy, Canada, and in the Bay of St. Malo on the north coast of

France. Both have maximum tidal ranges near 15 m. The tidal cycle is tied to the lunar month so that maximum tidal range, called *spring tide,* is at the new and full moon. The first and third quarter of the lunar cycle give us a minimum tidal range, the *neap tide* (figure 1.7).

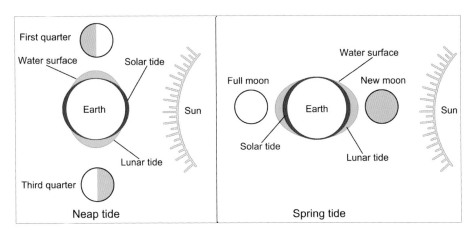

Figure 1.7
Diagram showing the sun, earth, moon relationships that produce lunar tides

Depending upon location, there can be two tidal cycles per day, called semi-diurnal tides or only one cycle per day, called diurnal tides (figure 1.8). In some places there is a combination of both situations, which are called mixed tides, meaning that some days the tide is diurnal and some days it is semi-diurnal. The Gulf of Mexico is an example of that. Because of the complexity of shorelines and the *nearshore bathymetry* (underwater topography), we can say that the tidal diversity around the globe is much like fingerprints. No two places are exactly the same.

There are also local tides that are caused by the wind friction over the water surface. In places where wind is brisk it is common for water level to be elevated or depressed depending on wind direction. These are called *wind tides.* The coast of Texas in the United States is a good example. On that coast the lunar tides are typically less than 0.5 m at many locations and the wind tides can commonly be that much or more. In large lakes where lunar tides are of no consequence, the wind tides can be major factors in beach dynamics. Setup from storms can cause water along the shoreline to rise as much as a meter. This can produce major erosion to the beach.

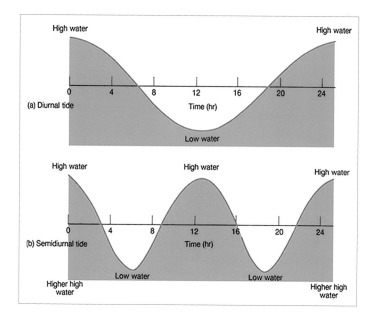

Storms create a special set of circumstances for the beach environment. A high level of energy is generated by strong wind that produces large waves and strong wave-generated currents. The intensity and frequency of storms varies considerably from place to place across the earth surface. The most intense of these are the *tropical storms* called *hurricanes* in the Western Hemisphere and *typhoons* in Asia and the Pacific. Actually, from the meteorological point of view, both of these are *cyclones.* A cyclone is a general term for circulation of an air mass that is counterclockwise in the Northern Hemisphere and clockwise in the Southern Hemisphere. Special terminology is applied depending on wind velocity. A tropical storm has a wind velocity of 34–64 knots (39–74 mph), and a hurricane or typhoon has a wind velocity of at least 65 knots (75 mph). (A knot is 1.852 km/hr or 1.0 nautical mph.)

These conditions produce huge waves that impact the beach and move considerable volumes of sediment. The strength of the wind, size of the waves, and the setup caused by the storm all contribute to changes produced by the storm. This is commonly called a *storm tide* or *storm surge* and can reach several meters. Wind velocity, storm movement, and offshore bathymetry are factors in generating the storm surge. The slower the storm progresses, the more the water level increases. A broad, gently sloping *continental shelf* such as offshore of Florida in the United States and Queensland in Australia will lead to high storm surge as compared to the steeper shelf along the Pacific coast of Mexico and Japan.

A single storm can erode a beach up to the entire volume of sediment making up the beach. This damage is caused by seaward and/or landward movement of the sand depending on the form and structure of the coast and the intensity of the storm. In many circumstances this damage is temporary because there are mechanisms that allow the beach processes to repair the damage and bring it back to or near its pre-storm condition. That does not always occur, however. It is most likely that eroded sand will return to the beach if the nearshore gradient is very gentle. In places where the nearshore is quite steep the eroded sand may be too deep for non-storm conditions to transport the sand back to the beach. This condition is especially common on the west coast of North America (figure 1.9).

The occupied beach experiences major negative impact from coastal storms, especially severe cyclones (hurricanes and typhoons). Because of its attractive location, construction is extensive on and near the beach. In many cases it is not well planned for such storms. The result is billions of dollars in loss and damage. In only a few days buildings, roads, and coastal structures such as *seawalls* and *jetties* can be heavily damaged.

MORPHODYNAMICS

The changes that are exhibited in surface coastal environments through time are called *morphodynamics,* which is essentially a series of cause and effect situations. Because of the continuous changes that the beach experiences, the amount of time involved can be as short as a tidal cycle or as long as decades. The changes can be somewhat subtle or very obvious. This discussion will begin with a description of beach and nearshore morphology and then cover how the changes take place in both time and space.

As stated, the beach is any shoreline accumulation of sediment regardless of its extent or its composition or grain size. Because

Figure 1.9
The coast of Oregon, USA, is a good example of a place where there is (right) an erosional winter beach, and (below) a summer beach with abundant sand.

the adjacent seaward nearshore environment is so intimately integrated with the beach, they are considered as a composite morphodynamic unit. The typical beach profile includes a back-shore dry beach, a foreshore, and the seaward nearshore zone of *longshore sandbars* and troughs (figure 1.10). The dry backshore tends to be nearly horizontal in orientation and may be a hundred or more meters wide—or it may not exist at all. The foreshore is the intertidal portion of the beach where waves rush up and back before they are stopped by the shoreline. After storms the entire *backbeach* may be eroded so the beach is only a seaward-dipping foreshore.

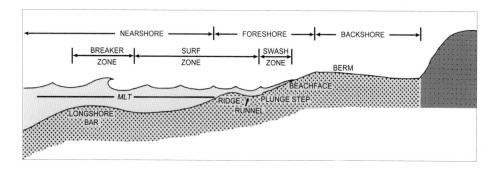

Figure 1.10
Diagram of the typical beach and nearshore profile

The nearshore zone varies from one location to another depending on the availability of sediment and the slope of the bottom. A major factor in this is the tectonic setting of the coast itself. Tectonics is the process whereby the earth's rocky plates move, both horizontally and vertically, over the planet's surface. The tectonic setting generally refers to two major types of motion of these lithospheric plates: 1) *collision coasts,* where adjacent crustal plates are moving toward each other; or 2) *trailing edge coasts,* where adjacent plates are moving away from each other. On trailing edge coasts there is commonly a coastal plain that has a broad, low-relief coast containing estuaries and barrier/inlet systems with a wide beach and nearshore zone and a gently sloping inner continental shelf. Good examples are the east coasts of North and South America. In contrast, collision coasts have high-relief coastal zones with a steep and narrow nearshore zone (figure 1.11). The upland is typically high in relief and may even have mountains adjacent to the shoreline. The beaches are commonly discontinuous with bedrock headlands. Examples are the west coasts of North and South America.

If sediment is not limited along the coast, the number of long-shore sandbars depends on the slope or gradient. The steep nearshore may have only one sandbar, or if it is very steep none may be present. Collision coasts commonly have no sandbars. Trailing edge coasts typically have multiple longshore sandbars, most commonly two or three (figure 1.12).

Dr. Andrew Short of the University of Sydney and his colleagues have created a terminology for the general nature of beach-near-shore profiles that is now widely used. It concerns the interaction

Figure 1.11
Collision coast with steep nearshore and no longshore sandbar

Figure 1.12
Trailing edge coast on the coast of Texas with multiple longshore sandbars with waves breaking over them

of waves with the overall profile steepness. A steep nearshore profile with few or no longshore bars permits a significant amount of wave energy to reach the shoreline due to water depth. Such beaches are termed *reflective* because a fair amount of wave energy is reflected off the steep beach. By contrast, a gentle nearshore gradient causes wave energy to dissipate and decrease as waves pass through the nearshore zone. These are the *dissipative* beaches.

Figure 1.13
Erosional beach
as it appears after
a storm with dark
heavy minerals in
the upper foreshore

Beach morphodynamics can be considered as being in two categories, eroding or prograding (building toward the water). First we will consider the eroding, or erosional, beach. Some combination of limited sediment, storms, and a steep nearshore tends to produce a narrow, steep, and erosional beach. This can occur as the result of a single storm (figure 1.13) and may be temporary, or it can be a chronic condition at a particular location. An erosional beach is nearly all foreshore and commonly has dark *heavy minerals* in the upper portion. These high-density minerals act as lag deposits, essentially *placers,* as the light minerals are carried away by the wave swash. This is also called a *storm beach profile.* It can be produced by a single storm and then recover, or it can persist. Commonly the erosional or storm profile will prevail during the winter because storms tend to be common and relatively intense during the winter.

In most locations the beach will recover from storm-generated erosion. Recovery can occur after a single storm if storms are widely spaced in time, or recovery can be in the spring as winter storm activity ceases (figure 1.9). The post-storm profile commonly includes what is called a *ridge and runnel.* This profile includes an accumulation in the form of a ridge that is a low sandbar composed of some of the eroded sediment from the beach and an intervening runnel that is essentially a shallow trough (figure 1.14). The entire ridge and runnel tends to be intertidal

Figure 1.14
Example of a ridge
and runnel unit at
low tide on the coast
of Lake Superior in
the United States

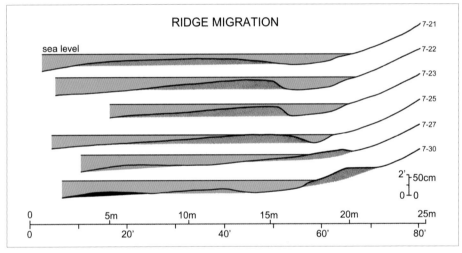

Figure 1.15
Diagram showing the
migration of a ridge
onto the storm beach
to replace sediment
that was eroded
during the storm that
produced the ridge

but may also form on coasts that are for practical purposes tideless, such as large lakes. Non-storm conditions permit the ridge to slowly migrate landward and eventually to weld onto the erosional beach surface thereby replacing sediment that was removed in the storm (figure 1.15). This does not always happen because another storm can occur before the ridge welds to the beach. Sediment is transported landward as wave-generated currents carry it across the ridge. The internal layering in the ridge shows thin strata that essentially parallel the landward-facing surface of the migrating ridge (figure 1.16).

Figure 1.16
Close-up showing
the stratification
of sediments in the
migrating ridge

The amount of time that it takes for the ridge to migrate on to the foreshore beach depends on various factors, including tidal range and slope of the ridge surface. On the larger tidal range coasts the landward migration of the ridge is very slow because it is exposed during much of the tidal cycle. In non-tidal places or on coasts were the tidal range is below a meter, this migration is relatively rapid because the ridge is submerged over much of the tidal cycle. It is under these conditions that the wave-generated current moves landward over the ridge surface. It is possible to stand on the ridge surface and watch the sand being carried landward. It reaches the landward margin and the sand cascades down the slope into the runnel. If another storm does not occur, this ridge will make its way up onto the foreshore beach and be re-worked into the beach by the swash of the waves as they surge up the foreshore.

Beach erosion may move sediment landward as well as seaward. Depending on the topography of the beach and adjacent landward environment, erosion may carry a large amount of sediment from the beach and transport it landward. This landward-transported sediment is typically deposited in the form of *washover fans*. Washover fans are generally thin and, as the name implies, shaped like a fan (figure 1.17). Very intense storms with a large storm surge can also excavate *washover channels* that lead to the washover fans from the back-

Figure 1.17
Post-storm conditions on a low barrier showing the presence of washover fans

Figure 1.18
Washover fans that extend into the back-barrier bay

beach. If the eroding beach is on a low and/or narrow *barrier island,* it is not uncommon for the fans to extend into the back-barrier bay (figure 1.18).

In the second type of beach morphodynamics, the progradational beach builds toward the water, that is, it accretes or grows. A progradational beach (figure 1.19) can be a chronic situation as long as sediment is continually available and storms are rare or modest in their intensity. This type of beach typically occurs along coasts where wave energy is low and storms are infrequent and of

Figure 1.19
Common appearance of a progradational beach with wide backbeach and incipient dunes called coppice mounds

low intensity. These conditions are present in the Gulf of Mexico, the Mediterranean Sea, and other places that are fetch-limited i.e. smaller than oceans. The combination of small waves and abundant sediment provides the conditions for long-term beach progradation.

This type of coast also tends to generate sand dunes. The wide dry backbeach is an excellent setting for onshore wind to blow sand landward. Any obstruction, especially plants, will cause this wind-blown sand to collect and form small accumulations. These are known as *coppice mounds* and they are the precursors to dunes. It is common for a progradational or accreting beach to have a profile with coppice mounds and foredunes landward of the dry beach (figure 1.20). In some places the dunes can exceed 10 m in height (figure 1.21).

Figure 1.20
Good example of a progradational beach with coppice mounds and foredunes on the Florida coast

Figure 1.21
High dunes that have accumulated by wind blowing onshore with a very large sand supply in Santa Catarina, Brazil

SUMMARY

The processes that influence beach dynamics are few, but they act in complicated ways along the shoreline, in somewhat of a domino fashion. The weather drives the wind that produces waves, and the waves can generate currents. All of these interact with the sediment, typically sand, to generate change on the beach. Some beaches are wide and flat, some are narrow, and others are combinations. Although the beach is a narrow strip of the earth's surface, it can be influenced by the largest scale features on the planet: crustal plates. Beach morphology is in part dependent on the location on a crustal plate and the type of motion that plate is experiencing. The main differences are between collision coasts (where the plates are moving toward each other) and trailing edge coasts (where the plates are moving away from each other).

Some folks might say if you have seen one beach you have seen them all. This is both true and false. No matter the location and setting of any individual beach, the same factors are driving its performance. On the other hand, no two beaches are exactly the same in size, shape, sediment, or energy level of the processes acting upon them. Not in dispute is the fact that the beach is dynamic and always fascinating.

2 Beach Materials

In many respects, the beach is a garbage can of materials. It includes mineral sediment, some organic materials, and unfortunately, a lot of garbage produced by beachgoers and boats. More about that later. The natural beach is comprised of rock and mineral fragments of all sizes, shapes, and compositions. When an individual is asked about a beach, the first thing that comes to mind is sand. Probably the second is waves. Sand is only one type of beach sediment. The origin of the sediment determines the composition of the beach, and the history of its transportation to the beach determines the size and shape of the particles. Sediment can be essentially anything that is not readily soluble (like salt). It is controlled by the rock and mineral composition of the rock from which it is derived or more directly from the coastal area adjacent to the beach.

Beach materials come from many locations: mountains (as many as thousands of kilometers away), nearby coastal plains, rolling hills, cliffs along the shore, the ocean floor (including reefs on the adjacent continental shelf), and from physical-chemical precipitation, especially organism skeletons. Movement of weather systems and drainage of streams provide much of the beach sediment, but waves and currents are also significant contributors. Sediment movement through various avenues to and from beaches goes on nearly continuously but with major pulses at certain times and under certain conditions. Floods from rain and/or melting snow can provide huge volumes of sediment, both sand and *mud,* to the coast. Typically most of the sand eventually reaches the beach and most of the mud is carried offshore, but some of both sizes come to rest on the *river delta.*

Once it reaches the shoreline, the sediment is moved by a combination of waves and currents. The size, and thus the energy, of the waves ranges widely in both time and space.

The same can be said for currents, and they can move in a wide range of speeds. The sediment on and near the beach can be made of particles of any size from only a few microns up to meters in diameter. Under some wave conditions very large sediment particles can be moved by either or both waves and currents, and under other conditions no sediment at all may be moved.

GRAIN SIZE

Beach sediments are classified by particle size. The grains-size scale was proposed by William Wentworth in 1922 and has persisted since then (table 2.1). As noted above, sediment particles occur in a huge range of sizes: from a few microns to meters in diameter. How do you categorize, in simple terms, such a range in sizes? Wentworth did it through the negative log to the base two of the diameter in millimeters:

$$-\log_2 x \text{ grain size(diameter in mm)}$$

In simple terms this says that adjacent categories are either double or half the size of the other. By size we mean the maximum diameter of the particle.

This approach reduces the categories to small whole numbers, both positive and negative, that are expressed with the phi symbol (ϕ). Sand is 1/16 mm (.0625) to 2.00 mm, which on the Wentworth Scale is +4ϕ to -1ϕ. This is commonly expressed verbally for the various categories such as very fine sand to very coarse sand, etc. (table 2.1). Most general conversations or publications about sediment, whether considering a beach or any other environment, use the terms mud, sand, gravel, boulders, etc. These are commonly used names for sediment, but they do have specific quantitative meanings (table 2.1). The *mean grain* size of beach sediment, or any other sediment for that matter, is determined and expressed in phi units also.

The grain size of beach sediments varies from very small to very large. There are mud beaches with very low wave energy on the coast of Surinam in South America, and on the other end of the spectrum there are beaches with huge boulders in many locations. The complete range in between is distributed all over

Table 2.1

Wentworth Grain Size Scale

Limiting particle diameter					
mm	φ units	Size class			
2048	-11	Very large			
1024	-10	Large	Boulders		
512	-9	Medium			
256	-8	Small			
128	-7	Large	Cobbles		
64	-6	Small			
32	-5	Very coarse	Pebbles	GRAVEL	
16	-4	Coarse			
8	-3	Medium			
4	-2	Fine			
2	-1	Very fine	Granules		
1	0		Very coarse		
1/2	+1	500 μm	Coarse	Sand	
1/4	+2	250 μm	Medium		
1/8	+3	125 μm	Fine		
1/16	+4	62 μm	Very fine		
1/32	+5	31 μm	Very coarse	Silt	MUD

the world. The geology of the coastal region is an important factor in determining the grain size.

It is also important to communicate in exact terms about other aspects of beach sediment, such as its uniformity of texture, which is called *sorting* (figure 2.1). This is also a statistical value, the standard deviation. It is also presented in phi units (ϕ). More simply, are the particles all about the same size (good sorting) or do they range widely (poor sorting)? There are specific values for each verbal category. The combination of mean grain size

Figure 2.1
A general diagram
of sediment particle
size distribution
showing a well-sorted
sediment (bottom)
and a poorly sorted
sediment (top)

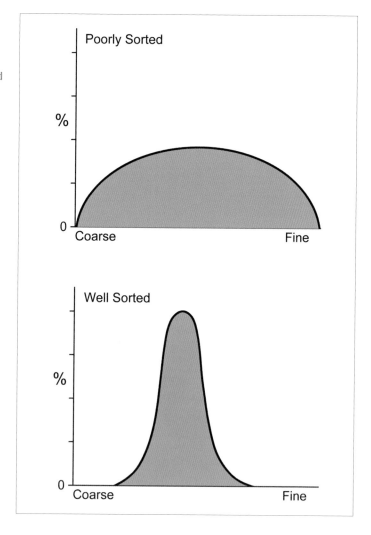

Figure 2.2
Close-up view
of well-sorted
beach sand

and sorting is the typical approach to describing sediment. This classification system applies to all depositional environments, not just beaches. Beaches tend to be well-sorted sand (figure 2.2), but there are differences (depending, of course, on multiple factors). Some beaches are boulders (figure 2.3).

Figure 2.3
Pocket beach
on Cape Ann,
Massachusetts,
USA, that is
dominated by
well-sorted
boulder gravel

There is a special sediment texture that we see on many beaches that doesn't quite fit the "well-sorted" sand category. It is also quite common, since many beaches have abundant shells. The typical beach sediment in these places is well-sorted sand combined with many shells and shell fragments. This sediment represents two origins: the sand from mineral and/or rock fragments that could have come from someplace far away from the beach, and the shell material that came from organisms that lived very near the beach, just offshore. Both sources look and are quite different. Each has its own set of grain-size parameters, and it is called a *bimodal sediment* (figure 2.4).

Figure 2.4
A general diagram
of sediment particle
size distribution
showing a bimodal
sediment

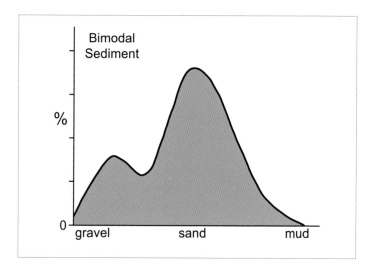

Bimodal sediments are common along the coasts of the world, wherever the beach sediment is derived from two origins or locations. Although the combination of sand and shells is the most common, it is not the only beach sediment that is bimodal. The base of cliffs may have large cobbles and boulders mixed with sand, Pacific islands may have reef debris mixed with volcanic sand, and beaches in northern high latitudes may have coarse glacial gravel mixed with sand. Other combinations also can occur.

Grain shape is also an important factor in characterizing sediment particles. This is especially important when considering shells or shell fragments that are incorporated into the beach

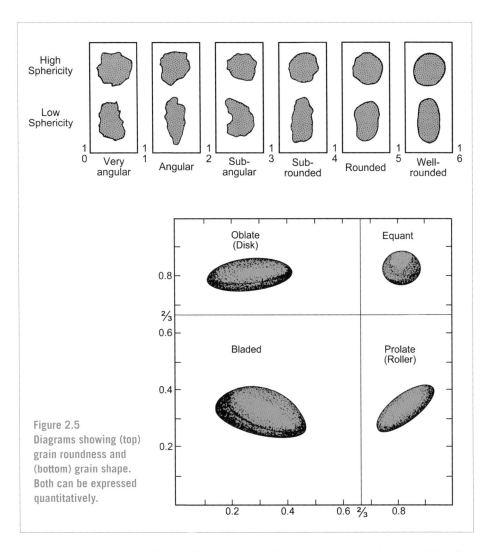

Figure 2.5
Diagrams showing (top) grain roundness and (bottom) grain shape. Both can be expressed quantitatively.

sediment. There are two three-dimensional characteristics that are commonly considered; roundness and sphericity. *Roundness* applies to the smoothing or rounding of the corners (figure 2.5 top). *Sphericity* is the approach to being equidimensional or approaching a sphere in shape (figure 2.5 bottom). For example, a hotdog is well-rounded but not spherical. Grain shape can also be described quantitatively, but numerical values are rarely used. Generally, descriptions such as angular, sub-rounded, rounded, and well-rounded are adequate.

For the most part the roundness of a grain is achieved as the particle is transported to the beach. A particle that is broken from an inland bedrock surface is tumbled and collides with other similar particles as it is transported by the wind or down a stream valley. This continual collision breaks off minute edges to smooth the surface of the particle and thereby generate a rounded grain. The same result can be achieved in the surf zone by continual wave action acting on the sand grains. Physical interactions of grains results in this smoothing of edges regardless of where, how, or how rapidly it takes place.

There are some sediment particles that have inherited shape factors. These especially influence the sphericity of a grain. This tends to be related to the crystallography of the mineral comprising the grain. Mica is probably the most common. It tends to break up into very thin sheets that never become spherical regardless of energy, time, or distance. The shape of these grains is controlled by their internal crystal make-up. On the other hand, some grains are inherently spherical. Carbonate sand grains called *ooids* are essentially all spherical because of how they form. Occasionally, ooids can fracture and lose their spherical shape since they are made of calcite, which is soft and chemically active at surface temperatures.

Grain shape may strongly influence the transportation of sediment particles. Those that are flat and disk-shaped may travel rather easily as they move like a feather within fluid, be it the atmosphere or the hydrosphere. The mica grains mentioned above are like that. Particles that are somewhat flat like bivalve shells may, however, be relatively difficult to pick up and initiate transport. Bivalve shells are commonly smooth and rounded on one side and cupped on the other. If the shell is lying on the bottom with the smooth side up, it will be much more difficult for a current to pick up and move, but if it is cup-side-up it will be relatively easy.

COMPOSITION

Just like grain size, the composition of the grains ranges widely. It can be almost anything that isn't soluble. The harder the better for sustainability on the beach but some sediment particles are soft. Minerals have a *hardness* scale that ranges from 1 to 10 called

Moh's Scale of Hardness. It is simply based on which material will scratch which. The scale ranges from talc (1) to diamond (10). Most beach sand is quartz, which has a hardness of 7. By contrast the shells are made of calcium carbonate, which is only a hardness of 3.

Sediment on the beaches comes from many places and is derived from rocks of many compositions. Just to give a few examples, let's start with granite, a common rock type in many mountainous areas. Granite is composed primarily of feldspar and quartz, two of the most common minerals exposed to erosion on the earth's surface. Quartz is almost inert at surface conditions but feldspar can experience physical and chemical weathering somewhat more easily. It is a hardness of 6, whereas quartz is 7. In addition, feldspar has *cleavage,* which is a crystallographic characteristic that allows it to break along planes of weakness. Quartz has no cleavage. These factors make quartz much more durable than feldspar. Although feldspar is more common in the earth's crust, quartz is much more common in beach sediment. It can withstand the time and rigors of travel from its mountain origin better than can feldspar.

If shells are composed of some type of calcium carbonate (calcite) and they are only a hardness of 3, why are there so many shells on some beaches? The reason is that the organisms that produced the shells lived close by. The close proximity of the shelled creatures eliminates the rigor of travel and the time it takes to reach the beach. If we take a sample of beach sand from a location where shells are common, you can be sure that there will be some sand-sized particles of calcium carbonate mixed in with the shells and predominantly quartz sand (figure 2.6). The nature of the shell material also is a factor in the lifetime of the calcium carbonate grains. Some shells are thin and fragile such as sand dollars and others are thick and massive like oysters.

Most beach sand is quartz, feldspar, and other rock fragments of various types. These three categories of silicate material plus shell debris comprise more than 95% of all beach sediment. In some locations, there can be a high percentage of other materials, the most common of which are volcanic in origin. In some places the

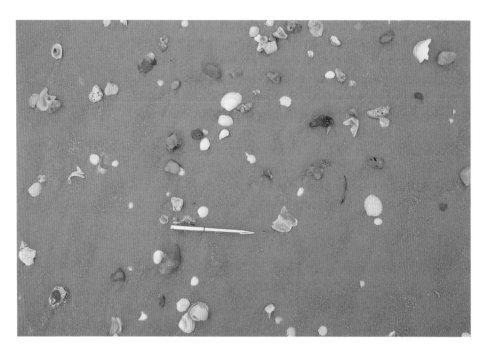

Figure 2.6
Close-up photo of
beach sand that is
composed of mixed
grains including
shell fragments

mineral magnetite (iron oxide) may comprise the entire beach (figure 2.7a). This occurs on the North Island of New Zealand, where the magnetite on the beach has been shipped to Japan for their steel industry. Dunes are even composed of magnetite on that island (figure 2.7b).

There are beaches that have small amounts of other minerals in their sediment, generally only a percent or two. Although only a small part of the total volume of the beach, these minerals may be quite important. In some parts of the world they are mined because of their special value. In general, these minerals are called heavy minerals because they have a high specific gravity. As a result, they behave differently as they are transported.

We all know that gold is quite a heavy mineral, about 14 times as heavy as water. Because of this characteristic, gold particles can rather easily be separated from other sediment particles. This is how "panning for gold" is done. Simply sloshing the sediment and water around in a shallow pan causes the much heavier gold particles to separate from the others and be collected for assay and sale. The heavy minerals that can accumulate in the beach

Figure 2.7
(a) Oblique photo of magnetite beach on the North Island of
New Zealand with a Jeep for scale, and (b) magnetite dune
in the same area with arrow pointing to a 6 inch scale

sediment are similar but much less heavy than gold. The magnetite mentioned above is an example. Additional heavy minerals are zircon, rutile, garnet, and others. Some of these are used as additives in paint, as abrasives on sand paper, and in other products. It only takes 1 to 3% by volume of heavy minerals to provide an economically viable mineral deposit.

There are commercial mining enterprises on land near the northwest coast of Florida in the United States, on the coast of Western Australia, and on the west coast of India, Indonesia, and other places. One of the good things about this type of mining is that very little of the sediment is removed for commercial use so that the terrain can be put back into its pre-excavation appearance without difficulty.

ORIGINS

The sources of beach sediment are many. They come from bedrock, glacial deposits, river beds, reefs, and organisms. Most beach sediments, the durable ones, come from erosion of bedrock through various processes. The weather is an important factor. The daily change from the highest to lowest temperature of a given rock can range up to 50°C, particularly in the desert. Minerals expand and contract as the temperature changes. These changes cause cracks in minerals and more commonly in rocks (which are aggregates of mineral grains). These cracks can fill with moisture that will freeze at low temperatures. The expansion as ice forms breaks rocks. Eventually particles small enough to move in a stream or river will start the trip toward a depositional basin such as a sea or ocean. Many other modes of physical breakdown can also take place. The simple falling of rock down a cliff or steep slope will "make little ones out of big ones."

Climate can also be a major factor in weathering. Moisture is the primary agent in chemical weathering. Water can combine with various elements to produce acidic compounds that react with minerals over very long periods of time to cause breakdown between rock fragments and within mineral grains. These very slow processes on the outcrop eventually produce sediment that can be transported to a coast where it may eventually reach a beach.

GLOBAL EXAMPLES

The variety of beaches throughout the world is enormous. They vary in grain size, composition, morphology, and extent—and, of course, in how they look and feel to the humans that visit them, and how much human development has altered them. In this chapter we will deal only with their measurable attributes. We can gain an appreciation of beach variety by considering some examples from around the world. The objective here is simply to provide the reader with a good appreciation of the variation in beach texture, composition, and morphology.

Spiekeroog, Germany The barrier islands along the North Sea coast of the Netherlands and Germany are short with wide, low, dissipative beaches. The sediment that comprises these barriers comes from glacial deposits of the ice sheets that covered Northern Europe during the *Pleistocene Epoch*. The tidal range here is 2.0–2.8 m producing a wide intertidal beach adjacent to the wide dry beach (figure 2.8a). These conditions produce very large ridge and runnel systems (figure 2.8b). The regional transport of sediment along these barrier beaches is toward the east and is substantial.

Figure 2.8a
The wide beach of fine sand on the island of Spiekeroog on the North Sea coast of Germany

Figure 2.8b
The same Spiekeroog
beach showing the
common shelters that
are used along this
coast

Bay of Fundy, Canada The Bay of Fundy is in Nova Scotia on the Atlantic coast of North America. Although this *estuary* is best known for its huge tidal ranges, it also has very interesting beaches These beaches range from boulders to very fine sand. The sediment in the boulder beaches (figure 2.9) does not move unless there is very high wave energy. These conditions take place during the winter storms that produce high velocity wind from the southwest that blows along the maximum fetch of the estuary. The boulders are derived from adjacent bedrock and from glacial moraines.

Figure 2.9
A boulder beach on
the east end of the
Bay of Fundy in
Nova Scotia, Canada.
The bedrock source
of these boulders
can be seen in the
background.

Figure 2.10
A coarse gravel washover at Cape Split in the Bay of Fundy

The intensity of wave energy in this estuary can cause gravel up to cobbles in grain size to washover the backbeach. Whereas we normally think of sand as a washover fan, here the presence of coarse gravel beaches coupled with the very high wave energy produces these cobble washovers (figure 2.10). These features are also at the east end of the bay taking advantage of the maximum fetch.

Bahamas The Bahama Bank is a thick sequence of calcium carbonate that has been accumulating east of the Florida Platform for many millions of years. The sediments here are a combination of skeletal debris, ooids, and lime mud. There are beaches throughout the numerous islands of the bank. These beaches can be wide and dissipative, and some are narrow, steep, and reflective. The wave energy is low except during tropical storms and hurricanes, and the tidal range is about 30 cm. Most of the beaches are composed of skeletal debris (figure 2.11). This sediment is made from a wide range of organisms (figures 2.12 and 2.13).

Figure 2.11
(a) Photo of Bahamas
carrbonate beach and
(b) close-up of
Bahamas beach sand

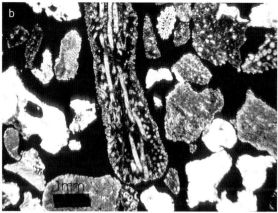

Figure 2.12
Low power photomi-
crographs showing
(left) angular skeletal
sediment and (right)
spherical ooids
that are common in
Bahamian sand

 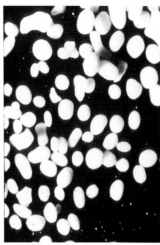

2.13
A barrier spit on
the Huelva coast
of southwest
Spain facing the open
Atlantic Ocean

Huelva, Spain The coast near Huelva in Spain is where Christo-
pher Columbus left on his voyage to the New World. The estuary
at La Rabida is the harbor from which he embarked. It is a
mesotidal coast with dissipative beaches that open to a low-energy
portion of the Atlantic Ocean (figure 2.13). The beaches are
well-sorted *terrigenous* sand (derived from land) with little shell,
although rock fragments occur locally (figure 2.14a). Tidal range
here is about 1.2–1.5 m, but the gently sloping beaches exhibit

Figure 2.14
Two beach
close-ups showing (a)
a steep but apparently
stable beach with
scattered course
rock debris, and (b) a
wide, gently sloping
intertidal beach, both
on the Atlantic coast
of Spain

a wide intertidal beach (figure 2.14b). The estuary drains the Rio Tinto mining region in the interior and a phosphate beneficiation plant at Huelva. Thus, the local water quality is very bad and the environment is essentially a biological desert except for *nekton*, swimming animals, during flood tides. The pH is commonly about 3—very acidic. The open ocean environment near the beaches has good water since the pollution does not reach the open water or is so diluted that it is not a problem.

Figure 2.15
A beach on the island of Hainan off the southern coast of China. The beach sediment is a mixture of shell debris (darker material) and terrigenous particles.

China Much of the China coast is bounded by tidal flats; beaches are not extensive. This is due to the combination of high tidal range and low wave energy on this dissipative coast. In addition most of the sediment delivered to the coast is very fine; sand is a minor component. There are local beaches bounded by bedrock headlands that are popular for recreation (figure 2.15). However, because of the high tidal ranges these are rather dangerous. Long ropes with floats are spaced across the beaches to provide safety for the swimmers to reach shore if they are in trouble.

Panama The south coast of Panama is nearly continuous with good beaches. The Pacific coast of Panama is unusual in that the tidal range is macrotidal even though it is a distinctly *wave-dominated* coast. This is typical of the Pacific coast of Central America with a reflective profile. The foreshore is steep and reaches across the entire tidal range, which can reach 6 m (figure 2.16a). The composition of these beaches is quite varied. There is a large component of metallic mineral and rock grains that are derived from the volcanic rocks in the interior only a few kilometers from the coast (figure 2.16b).

Figure 2.16
The macrotidal
Pacific coast of
Panama can have
(a) a more gently
sloping and
dissipative intertidal
beach and (b) a wave-
dominated, reflective
beach, although
the tidal range is
more than 6m. The dark
grains in (a) are from
volcanic rocks that
cropout nearby.

Brazil The coast of much of Brazil is dominated by beaches and large dunes. This changes a bit near the Amazon Delta where to the west the coast is dominated by mud. The mud is provided by the Amazon River and is carried both offshore and alongshore, primarily to the west. It is the source of the muddy part of the Surinam coast. East and south of the river, the coast has sand beaches and dunes that exceed 30 m high. The sand beaches

Figure 2.17
The beaches of Brazil
are generally stable
to progradational and
composed of medium,
well-sorted sand
whether they are
(a) in a metropolitan
area of Forteleza or
(b) adjacent to a
fishing village on the
coast of the State
of Ceara.

are important for recreation in the large cities and the small fishing villages. These beaches are mainly medium sand and have little shell debris (figure 2.17). The wave energy is modest and the mean tidal range is about 2.5 m (mesotidal).

Galapagos Islands The Galapagos Islands are in the Pacific Ocean off the coast of Ecuador. They are of volcanic origin like the other islands in this ocean. These islands are near the equator, with steep nearshore profiles and extensive reefs near their coasts. The steep and narrow beaches are composed of both volcanic and skeletal reef debris (figures 2.18). The grain size ranges from sand through boulder-size gravel (figure 2.19) with the volcanic material extending across all grain sizes and the skeletal material being sand and fine gravel (figure 2.20).

Figure 2.18
Some Galapagos beaches are fine gravel that is shell debris with abundant sea urchin spines.

Figure 2.19
Other Galapagos beaches have a composition of volcanic boulders.

Figure 2.20
Some of the Galapagos beaches are white skeletal sand derived from nearby reefs.

Figure 2.21
The Coramandel Peninsula of the North Island of New Zealand has fairly steep beaches because of the high wave energy. The high latitude prohibits reef debris.

North Island, New Zealand The Coromandel Peninsula of the North Island of New Zealand is a collision coast with high relief and a and a and a steep nearshore. The tides are semi-diurnal with about a 2.0 m range. The beaches tend to be reflective and beautiful (figure 2.21). This part of New Zealand is close to the tectonic plate boundary, and there are active volcanoes that are visible from shore.

Figure 2.22
The Skaelling Peninsula of Denmark on the North Sea coast showing (a) dunes in the background with (b) a well-developed ridge and runnel at low tide

Skaelling, Denmark The Danish west coast borders the North Sea. Included are multiple barrier islands, the northernmost of which is Skaelling near the coastal city of Esberg. This is a wave-dominated barrier that experiences mesotidal conditions and high wave energy. There are wide beaches, commonly with a ridge and runnel present, as well as front modest dunes that are stabilized by vegetation (figure 2.22a). Because of the mesotidal range here, the ridge and runnel can be quite wide (figure 2.22b). This site was where Nazi German armies had installations during World War II. Old bunkers, paved roads for tanks, and some munitions are still present. The University of Copenhagen has maintained and operated a field station on Skaelling since 1930. It was abandoned during World War II but reactivated thereafter and is still a thriving educational and research facility.

Arctic Sea Coast The Arctic coast near the Alaska-Canada border is characterized by permafrost, which is permanently frozen soil and substrate. The current situation with climate change is causing problems along this coast because the warming conditions are causing the permafrost to melt. A team of researchers from Potsdam University in Germany is investigating this situation. We can see slumping of coastal topography (figure 2.23) and much reworking of sediment that is primarily glacial drift that has been frozen for literally thousands of years.

Figure 2.23
Slumping of melting permafrost along
the Arctic Ocean coast of Alaska

Figure 2.24
Sand and gravel
beach on the
north shore of
Alaska on the
Arctic Ocean.
There is a person
for scale and
the white mass
is ice.

The beaches along the Arctic Ocean are rather wide and are comprised of a spectrum of glacially deposited sand and gravel (figure 2.24). This sediment has been reworked from the glacial deposits by the modest waves of this coastal environment during the summer only, when the coastal ice has melted. This area is a good place from which to demonstrate the existence of global warming. The U.S. Geological Survey has been monitoring ice-free conditions along this shoreline and finds that the number of days has increased from 80 in the 1980s to 140 at the present time.

SUMMARY

The beaches of the world are a really mixed bag of appearances. Some are short, some are long, some are wide and some are narrow, some have rock cliffs at their landward boundary, while others grade into extensive, virtually featureless plains. The composition of the beaches ranges widely and reflects source materials that are nearby or that have traveled via rivers from thousands of kilometers away. Particle size and shape is a reflection of the physical energy of waves and currents, plus to some extent the composition of the particles. Time is also a factor in the shape. Take a minute the next time that you visit a beach to look at the size, shape, and composition of its material and features.

3 Sea-Level Change and the Beach

The final process that we will consider is sea-level change, the slowest process that influences beaches. For the past several thousand years sea level has been rising nearly all of the time. There are only two reasons for sea level to change: the volume of water in the oceans changes or the size of the basins themselves changes. The latter takes place as the result of *plate tectonics* and is a very slow process, millions of years. Changing the volume of water can take place more quickly, in centuries or even decades. Earth is 4.6 billion years old, and sea level has been changing throughout that time. The size and shape of both the ocean basins and the continents have also been changing over that period.

As a few examples, we can look at *paleogeographic maps* of the globe to see some of the extreme changes in sea level relative to the landmasses. These maps are the result of the excellent and diligent work of Prof. Ronald Leakey at Northern Arizona University. He has spent most of his career collecting data and formulating maps for the entire geologic history of the globe. The major changes of the oceans and continents mean that the beaches were changing as well. The nature of the beach environment has not changed, but the distribution of beaches has varied greatly through time. The Cretaceous Period, which was the end of the time that dinosaurs inhabited the earth, about 65 million years ago, was a time when sea level was extremely high relative to the present (figure 3.1). At this time the length of the global coast was very much longer than at present, meaning that the length of the beach environment was similarly longer. This was also a time when Earth's climate was quite warm, more so than at present.

After the Cretaceous, the passage of time saw the continents increase in size and the length of the beaches decrease because the shoreline was reduced (figure 3.2). By the Late Miocene Epoch in the Tertiary Period, about 6 million years ago, the distribution of land and oceans was pretty similar to the present.

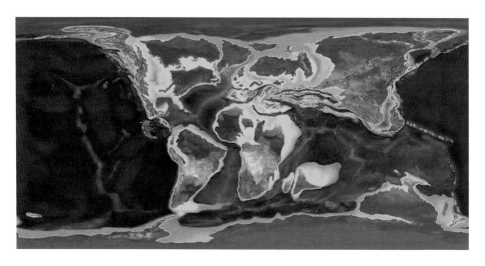

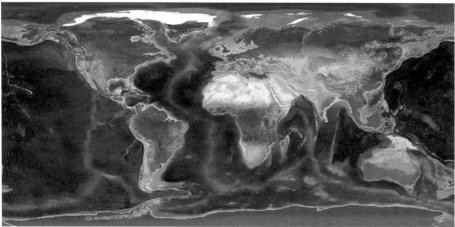

Figure 3.1
(Top) Paleogeography of the earth during the Late Cretaceous Period, about 65 million years ago. Huge shallow seas occupied North America and Eurasia along with many more *mediterraneans*.

Figure 3.2
(Bottom) Paleogeography of the earth during the Late Miocene Epoch about 6 million years ago. The general distribution of land and oceans is similar to the current situation.

The *Quaternary Period* of geologic time includes the past 2.6 million years. This has been a period of multiple glaciations. Climate change occurred in cycles of many thousands of years each (figure 3.3). Each one of the cycles included an extended time of glaciers that covered the mid- to high latitudes. That means that in the Northern Hemisphere much of North America, Europe, and Asia were glaciated. Those glaciers contained thousands of cubic kilometers of water, all of which came from the oceans. As a result, the oceans were much lower, as much as 125 m (410 ft). When the warm portion of the climate cycle approached, the glaciers melted and sea level rose about that much.

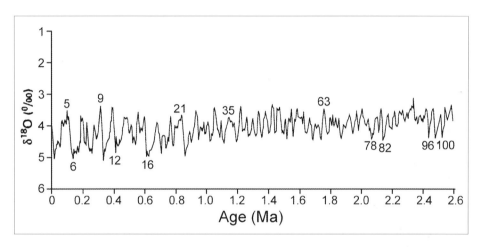

Figure 3.3
Oxygen isotope cycles during the 2.6 million years of the Quaternary Period. These are good proxies for climate change and therefore for sea-level change.

We are primarily interested in the last portion of the most recent climate cycle. At the time of maximum glaciation the present continental shelves of the world were part of the coastal plain (figure 3.4). Rivers extended across this relatively flat topography and deposited their sediment discharge down the continental slope. River deltas were not developed because the shallow marginal environment for sediment accumulation was not present. There were beaches between the river mouths that looked and behaved much like those of the present time.

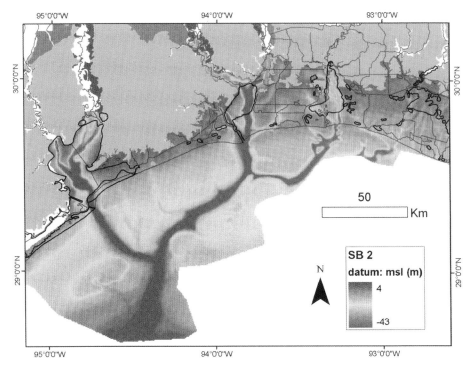

Figure 3.4
Paleogeography of what was the coastal plain with drainage systems, about 20,000 years ago. Sea level was much lower and the current continental shelf was exposed.

Glaciers have been melting for almost the past 20,000 years. This has added tremendous volumes of water to the oceans, enough to raise sea level more than 100 m (328 ft). As sea level began to rise, the shoreline moved landward and the beach environment moved with it. For the first few thousand years this happened at a rate much greater than the present rate, about 10 mm per year as compared to the present global rate of about 3 mm per year (figure 3.5). This rate was too rapid to establish significant wave-dominated coastal morphology with extensive beaches and barrier islands like we see today. Tidal processes dominated the coast. Beaches were present but were being washed over and destroyed for lack of significant sediment volume and enough time of stable sea level for coastal development.

These conditions characterized the continental margins of the world until about 7,000 years before present. The rapid rise in sea level slowed (figure 3.5) and the landward movement of the shoreline decreased enough so that wave processes were now dominating and beaches became common and extensive. This was the time that the coastal morphology as we know it began

Figure 3.5
Curve showing
sea-level rise
though time since
the last major
period of glaciation

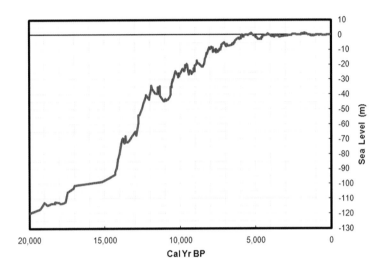

to form. Estuaries, river deltas, and barrier islands with extensive beaches became common throughout the low-relief coasts (figure 3.6). Although each of the four panels in this illustration shows the presence of beaches, it was not until about 7,000 to 6,000 years before present that these environments became established. By that time barrier islands were developing and beaches dominated the open shoreline.

The past 3,000 years have been a time of relative stability in sea level. Most of the modern active barriers have been formed or at least have been modified during this time. There is not agreement, however, as to the details of sea level during this period. Three scenarios have been suggested and championed: 1) sea level has reached its present position and remained so during that time, 2) sea level has risen very slowly over this period, or 3) sea level has risen and fallen one or two meters in multiple cycles during that time. There are some data that support each of these conditions.

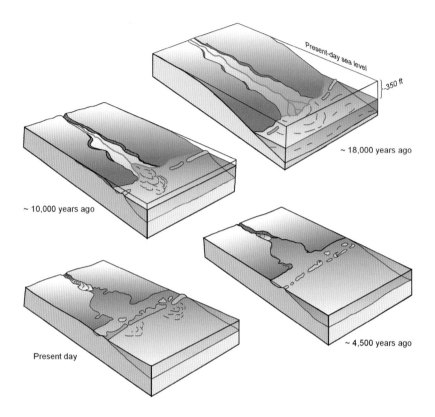

Present-day sea level

~350 ft

~ 18,000 years ago

~ 10,000 years ago

~ 4,500 years ago

Present day

**Figure 3.6
Schematic diagrams
showing stages
of coastal develop-
ment as sea level
rose during the Late
Quaternary**

Regardless of the actual sea level behavior over the past several centuries, we have a pretty good grasp of what has been going on over the past 100+ years. The best historic approach to measuring and monitoring sea level is through recording *tide gauges* We know from the tidal conditions and predictions that tides are essentially like fingerprints; no two locations are the same. Each site along the coast of the world experiences a different tidal pattern if the details of the record are considered.

The tide gauges must be placed where the substrate is stable, and this is nearly impossible due to sediment compaction. The best approach is to try to base the measuring device on bedrock. There are many places where that is not possible. It is now possible to measure tides with great accuracy from satellites. Weather also influences water level and setup or *setdown* from wind. Storm surge must be removed from astronomical tidal records. Nevertheless, it is possible to get trends and annual rates of sea level change from good tide gauges.

Looking around the globe it is possible see that there are places where sea level is actually falling. There are two major reasons for this: 1) plate tectonics, where there is movement along plate boundaries such as along the Pacific coast of North and South America, and 2) *isostatic rebound* from glacial melting, which is still occurring most notably in Scandinavia. Plate boundary areas experience earthquakes where movement along faults can be multiple meters in only seconds. This can cause a beach to be submerged and delivered to a different environment or it can elevate a beach above sea level and do the same. This happened in the Alaskan earthquake of 1964 (figure 3.7). The situation shown in figure 3.7 is along the Hanning Bay fault on Montague Island in Prince William Sound, Alaska. The shoreline and its included beaches moved up more than four meters in a matter of minutes. Similar changes took place in other parts of the Alaskan coast.

Figure 3.7
Aerial photo of the coastal uplift at the Hanning Bay fault on Montague Island in Prince William Sound, Alaska, USA

In the case of isostatic rebound, the huge ice mass of the glaciers caused the crust to be depressed, much like what happens when you get into a canoe: It goes down due to your weight. When you get out, the canoe rises again on the water surface. The ice mass causes the same effect on the crust, and its melting produces the same results. It is still happening in some of the higher latitudes of the Northern Hemisphere. A good example is along the Scandinavian coast where sea level is still falling. The emergence of the shoreline can also be seen on the margins of Hudson Bay, Canada, where multiple shorelines are preserved above the present one (figure 3.8).

Figure 3.8
Beach ridges on the margin of Hudson Bay, Canada, that indicate the lowering of sea level after glacial melting

Data from all sources show that current global annual sea level rise averages nearly 3 mm, but there are data that suggest that the rate is increasing and will continue to increase through this century. Sea-level change is one of the primary avenues of investigation by the Intergovernmental Panel on Climate Change (IPCC). This group has published multiple major reports, including 2000, 2007, and most recently 2014. According to IPCC, the intermediate rate of the mean predicted sea level change through the 21st century is about a half-meter (figure 3.9). If sea level does increase that amount by the end of the century, what will be the overall effect globally on the beach environment? Briefly, not much!

There are data now that show that the global rate of *sea-level rise* is increasing (figure 3.10). The problem is that we cannot tell if this increase is just a small, short-term phenomenon or if it is the beginning of a long-term trend. We know from various types of

Figure 3.9
Predictions of
sea-level rise by the
Intergovernmental
Panel on Climate
Change (IPCC) in its
2014 report

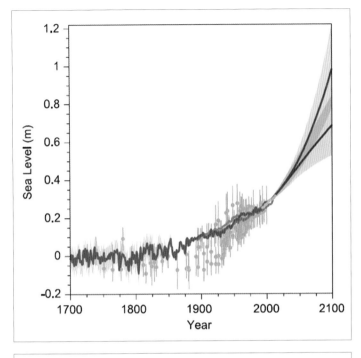

Figure 3.10
Recent data showing
that the rate of
sea-level rise has
increased during
the latter part
of the 20th century

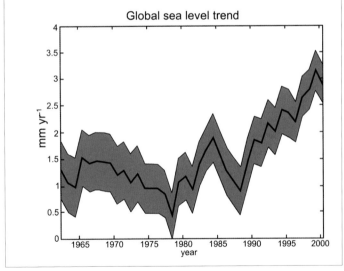

information that rates of change of sea level varied greatly over
only decades in the past. It is possible that the same situation is
occurring now.

PROBLEMS FOR BEACHES

Increasing sea level can cause problems for the beach environment, but the rates and the total amount predicted by IPCC are not likely to have a significant impact on beaches in most places. If we look at the median of the predicted rise, it amounts to only 50 cm spread over a century (figure 3.9). That is 5 mm/yr, which is twice the current global rate. Any rate up to and even a bit higher can be accommodated by most of the world's beaches for some decades. There are some beach morphologies that cannot experience this rate of sea-level rise without difficulties. Some shoreline regions where tides of two or more meters of tidal range are spread across a very gently sloping dissipative beach will experience some shoreline retreat. The availability of sediment is also a significant factor. Leading edge coasts where drainage systems are small typically deliver little sand-size sediment to shoreline.

The real problem for beaches is where the rate of sea-level rise is at a centimeter or more each year. There are places where this occurs now and the beaches cannot be sustained. The high rate of sea level rise and the scarcity of available sediment result in erosion of the beaches and the eventual destruction of barrier islands.

There is another important change that can take place over the present century. There are data to support the concept of climate change. This climate change is now in the form of global warming. Changes are expected in the weather accompanying this change in climate. One aspect of this is that various weather conditions will increase in intensity. Summers will be hotter and winters will be colder. Storms will be more severe than at present. It is this latter condition that can cause a negative impact on beaches. Stronger storms and possibly more frequent hurricanes will produce more extensive and more severe erosion on the beaches. Sediment delivery to the coast has been greatly reduced due to many dams on rivers and decreases in river discharges due to dry conditions in many areas. It is possible that some of these storms could destroy some beach environments and barrier islands.

REGIONAL AND LOCAL DIFFERENCES

There are many places in the world where there are significant differences in sea-level change from the global average. The majority of these differences can be attributed to the differences in the geology of the coast in the vicinity of the shoreline. This is typically related to the amount and rate of compaction in the strata that underlie the shore area. These strata may be comprised of sand, mud, or bedrock, especially limestone. The fluvial complexes and river deltas tend to be dominated by mud and sand. Mud sediment can contain more than 75% by volume of water. As this mud is buried, there is compaction caused by the overburden and this causes much, sometimes most, of the water to be released. This reduces the volume of the sediment, causing the sediment surface to be lowered and *relative sea level* to increase. The large deltas of the world are the sites of the highest rates of sea-level rise, and their barriers and beaches can be destroyed by the end of the century. The channel deposits are dominated by sand, which does not compact as much as the mud, but it also comprises much less area compared to the muddy deposits.

By contrast the coastal areas where bedrock is dominant experience little or no compaction, so sea level change tends to be maintained at or less than the global average. The most extensive coastal areas where this condition exists are where the carbonate platforms are located. The most well known of these are Mexico's Yucatan Peninsula and the Florida Peninsula of the United States. There is another condition that causes sea level to change differently than the global average. This is the tectonic setting of the coast in question. Two general settings are subject to this condition: coasts at or near plate boundaries and coasts on many oceanic islands. Movement along plate boundaries may cause the shoreline to be raised or lowered slowly through time or rapidly during an event such as an earthquake. As an example, the shoreline experienced more than a meter of sea-level change during the Alaskan earthquake of 1964 (figure 3.11). As much as four meters of relative sea-level change took place at some locations. A more recent situation in Japan was the earthquake of 2011 that saw sea level rise by 0.5–0.8 m in six minutes.

**Figure 3.11
Scarp formed
by the Alaskan
earthquake in
March, 1964**

By contrast, the islands on the oceanic lithosphere experience a different kind of sea-level change. These islands are very thick piles of volcanic material resting on a thin layer of oceanic lithosphere composed of the same lithology as the islands. The mass of the island is such that it causes *subsidence* in the same way that a thick glacier causes subsidence; it is an isostatic adjustment. The result is that relative sea level on the island shoreline is greater than the global average. There is considerable range from one island to another. Because the islands do not produce large and thick beaches due to lack of sediment discharge, the beaches are in jeopardy.

The most susceptible areas for beaches to experience problems with sea-level rise are on and near the large fluvial deltas. The Nile and Mississippi, for example, have deltas with significant wave-dominated coastal reaches as well as barrier islands with extensive beaches (figures 3.12a, 3.12b). These barriers are quite vulnerable to destruction because of the high rate of sea-level rise—on the order of a centimeter per year, more than three times the global average. This high rate is the result of the combined effects of compaction of delta sediments with the global rate of rise. As a consequence, these low elevation barriers are washed over during severe storms, causing the beach sediment

Figure 3.12a
Infrared satellite
image of the
Mississippi Delta
showing long and
narrow barrier
islands in the left
central portion
of the image.
These barriers
were formed by
waves reworking
abandoned
lobes of the delta.

Figure 3.12b
Wide beaches that have developed
on barrier islands of the Mississippi Delta

**Figure 3.13
Sequence of
maps showing the
destruction of
the Isle Dernieres
barrier island
complex as
sea level rose
over the past
about 150 years**

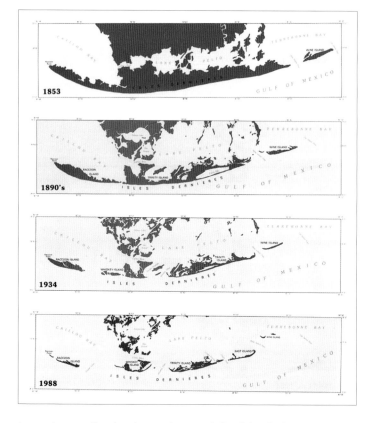

to wash over the barrier and spread the islands into thin sand sheets. A study by the United States Geological Survey shows that Isle Dernieres on the Mississippi River Delta has decreased tremendously over the past 150 years (figure 3.13). If this trend continues, these barriers and their beaches may be gone by the end of the century.

The Nile Delta is also experiencing similar conditions but for somewhat different reasons. Erosion on the outer coast beaches of the delta is severe both in terms of the high rate of sea-level rise and the huge reduction of sediment reaching the Mediterranean coast. The construction of the Aswan Dam to provide water to parts of Egypt some decades ago essentially stopped significant discharge of sediment to the delta. As a result, the combination of rising sea level with little or no new sediment being delivered to the coast has caused the current erosive situation.

Another human-generated cause-and-effect problem related to increased subsidence and erosion on deltas is the extraction of huge volumes of petroleum products that are being taken from beneath the surface of these deltas. In addition to the Mississippi, this is also occurring on the Niger Delta in western Africa. Like the Mississippi, the Niger Delta has very high petroleum production. The combination of climate change and petroleum withdrawal is likely to increase sea level 30 cm in the next 30 years and 110 cm in the next century. That is an average of 10 mm/yr, similar to that of the Mississippi. The consequences are expected to be the same.

Although a *tide-dominated* delta, the Ganges-Brahmaputra Delta in Bangladesh does have extensive beaches, though they are not associated with barrier islands. This huge delta is home to more than 140 million people in an area of nearly 90,000 square kilometers (37,000 mi^2). It is also a major agricultural region. The composition of the sediments is sand and mud, and compaction is a problem. Some areas of the delta are experiencing sea-level rise up to 25 mm per year, nearly 10 times the global average. The average along the open coast is about 8 mm per year.

Unlike the Mississippi Delta, a huge amount of sediment is delivered to the shoreline area on the Ganges-Brahmaputra River Delta on the Bay of Bengal in the Indian Ocean. Floods during the monsoon season are legendary. The discharge of both water and sediment is enormous during these events. Thousands of people drown, many more are displaced, and agricultural lands are flooded. These events transport so much sediment to the coast that the delta is growing seaward and beaches are increasing in size. A good example is shown in Figure 3.14, where the beach sand has accumulated as the tree-covered surface subsided with the compaction of sediment and the global rise in sea level. The photo shows tree stumps buried by beach sand with a gently sloping foreshore. Normally such a photo suggests erosion, but all data from a study by Dr. Steven Goodbred of Vanderbilt University shows that erosion is not a problem along this part of the coast.

Figure 3.14
Photo of a sand
beach on the outer
shoreline of the
Ganges-Brahmaputra
Delta showing tree
stumps left from
the buried coastal
forest

Not all coastal situations are experiencing above normal rates of sea-level rise. Because the geology is a major factor in subsidence and therefore in the rate that sea level is rising, it is important to know the nature of the strata at the coast. As was pointed out above, fine sediment with abundant moisture will lose that moisture, causing subsidence. By contrast, solid bedrock provides a stable elevation because there is no compaction. The best examples of this condition are associated with the Florida and Yucatan Platforms, which are large and thick deposits of limestone. Although limestone is fairly soluble and tends to form caves and sinkholes, the limestone itself does not compact or subside. As a result, rate of sea-level rise may be slower here as compared to most of the globe (figure 3.15).

Those coastal areas where rapid subsidence is accompanied by sea-level rise are at one end of the sea-level change spectrum and geologically stable substrates are at the other. The carbonate platforms of the Bahamas and Yucatan are among the most stable regions on the earth surface. They are removed from tectonically active areas and they are composed of limestone.

Figure 3.15
Tide gauge records for several decades showing trends and rates of sea-level rise

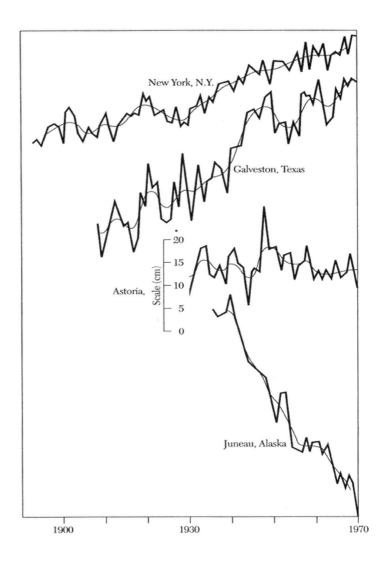

Beaches on these platforms are pure calcium carbonate, mostly skeletal debris. In places where there is limestone rock at or near the shoreline, there is commonly a small beach and sometimes there will be a notch at the present level of the sea (figure 3.16). These sea-level notches are the result of bio-erosion, generally by boring algae. They take a rather long time to form. Their location at present sea level indicates that the sea level has changed very little.

Figure 3.16
Notch in limestone
in the Bahama
Bank province, an
indicator of the
position of sea
level for a period
of time

SUMMARY

Changing sea level can cause problems for beaches, but in some cases it may also not be a problem, depending on location. In general, the underlying geology is a major factor in controlling how the beach behaves in our presently changing sea level. The tectonic setting is important, as is demonstrated by plate boundaries where relative sea level is rising in some places and falling is others. The most stable settings for relative sea-level rise are over carbonate platforms or other bedrock substrates. The places where the biggest problems exist are where the beach overlies thick, muddy sediment sequences such as fluvial deltas.

4 Human Influence on Beaches

The human species has always carried out activities to modify our environment. Beaches are no exception. This has been going on since the dawn of civilization. In the earliest days people who lived on the open coast did so primarily for two reasons: food and transportation. Both of these caused them to make some changes in the shoreline environment, which was typically a beach. To be sure, these modifications were quite modest. Various approaches to capturing fish were undertaken, generally the construction of some types of traps and holding areas. Most transportation was by small vessels that could be pulled up on the beach above high tide and then pushed back into the water when the need occurred. Modest places to moor larger boats were constructed at or near the shoreline in order to keep the vessels safe from storms. None of these modifications of the beach and nearshore caused significant changes to the beach or its incident processes. These modest structures caused some modification of waves and longshore currents that would influence sediment transport, but the results would not cause appreciable changes in beach morphology.

As time passed and inhabitants of the shoreline increased and became more concentrated, efforts to modify and control coastal dynamics became more extensive and more sophisticated. The main effort was to control erosion. Recall that sea level has been rising for almost 20,000 years. All significant occupation of the coast has taken place during the last few thousand years of that period. Erosion control efforts have been the focus of human influence on the shoreline for much of that time. These efforts began as simple protection of the shoreline, generally in the form of fortifications for military protection. They have become quite sophisticated, with engineering principles over the past century or so as the main approach to these efforts.

For the most part, some type of structure has been the approach to shoreline protection and stabilization. Some of these structures are on the shoreline, some are landward of it, and others are seaward. The structures can be composed of various materials. More recently so-called soft approaches to shoreline preservation have become very common. Beach nourishment is now prevalent on a global scale.

STRUCTURES

Waves and currents are responsible for changing the shoreline and the adjacent beach. Protecting and stabilizing the beach requires keeping those processes from interacting in a destructive way with the beach sediment. That simply means putting something in their path that prevents erosion from happening. This has historically been the approach. The most basic way to accomplish this is to place large rocks along the shoreline. Originally construction consisted pretty much of random placement of various sizes of boulders along the shoreline, an easy and inexpensive approach. Now it is done with a plan in place. Boulders are all set individually by size so that they will be in their most stable position to resist storms. The sizes of the boulders are considered based on expected wave energy. This type of material is generally called *rip rap* or *revetment* (figure 4.1). An advantage, in addition to the relative cost of such structures, is that rip rap structures have a very rough surface that allows some dissipation and absorption of wave energy. The most common use of the rip rap type structures is in a shoreline or backbeach location where it can take the direct impact of the waves. There are other locations where these structures are also placed. They can be offshore as *breakwaters* or as perpendicular *groins* along the shoreline.

Poured concrete is also a common type of structure for coastal applications. This can take on a variety of configurations, the most common of which is a simple vertical structure called a seawall. Some variations are also used. One is to curve the seaward surface to absorb some of the incident wave energy. Another method of absorbing some of the wave energy is to pour a stair-step shape on the seaward side. The previously described concrete structures are utilized at the shoreline or the backbeach. The simple vertical concrete structure can also be placed out in the nearshore for various protective purposes.

Figure 4.1
A rip rap and seawall structure designed to protect the beach

Sheet-piling is the other main type of material used in hard structures. It is long "plank-like" material that is interlocking and buried in the substrate vertically to present a hard, smooth surface to wave attack (figure 4.2). Sheet-piling can be made of steel, fiberglass, or vinyl. The value of the latter two materials is their resistance to corrosion in salt water. The type of structure can be placed essentially anywhere on land or in shallow to moderate water depths.

Figure 4.2
Sheet piling material of metal provides an interlocking structure to stop wave attack.

SHORE-PARALLEL STRUCTURES

Multiple types of protective structures are placed parallel to the shoreline. The most common is the seawall, which is pretty much what the name suggests. It is a wall constructed of any of the materials mentioned above and typically placed at the shoreline. These walls can be quite large and long structures that rise multiple meters above the substrate. Their main purpose is to protect upland buildings, roads, infrastructure, and so on from destruction caused by coastal erosion, primarily due to storms. The most landward of these are located at the edge of the active beach. This approach to coastal protection has both positive and negative impacts. Such structures generally do a good job of saving the upland community from destruction, but the beach adjacent to the wall is typically removed by erosion.

One of the problems of seawalls is that they can be undermined by erosion, causing them to topple over. This can be alleviated by including *tiebacks* to hold the wall in place even if much sediment is removed. The tieback is a steel rod that is anchored to a "deadman," generally a large piece of concrete that is buried behind the wall (figure 4.3). Inclusion of tiebacks is now a requirement for most permits for seawall construction.

Figure 4.3
A seawall that has its tie-downs exposed

A significant problem with seawalls is that they are generally vertical and reflect all of the incident wave energy. The long-term result of this battering is the failure of the structure. Any type of construction that absorbs or dissipates wave energy will prolong the functional life of the structure. One of the most successful seawalls in the world is the Galveston Seawall in Galveston, Texas, USA. In 1900 a severe hurricane destroyed the city and killed 8,000 people. In order to prevent another disaster of that magnitude, a seawall about 15 km long was constructed, with completion in 1904 (figure 4.4). This structure has stood the test of time and multiple hurricanes, the last of which, Hurricane Ike, was in 2008. It has a curved surface and protection on the base where wave run-up occurs. Coastal engineers consider this seawall one of the seven coastal structure wonders of the world!

Figure 4.4
Galveston seawall showing the curved face designed to absorb and dissipate wave energy

Shore-parallel structures placed in the water fall under the general term breakwater. These structures have similar construction to a seawall except that tie-downs are not possible. There are two main purposes of breakwaters. One purpose, as the name implies, is to break up the wave energy that is moving shoreward and thereby protect the beach. A common approach is to have multiple discontinuous breakwaters, thus allowing some wave energy to reach the shore. This commonly permits some transport and accumulation of sediment on the shoreline. The result is a series of *salients*—sediment accumulations behind these breakwaters that produce

a shoreline with regular protuberances (figure 4.5). Another purpose of breakwaters, especially those that are continuous, is to provide shelter from waves for mooring vessels.

The most common material for breakwater construction is rip rap, because of the relative ease of construction in water. It may be in a variety of forms, including bins of large boulders that protect the coast (figure 4.6). Another advantage of rip rap is that it absorbs wave energy much better than poured concrete or sheet piling. That is not to say that those two materials are not used, but they are less common in breakwaters.

Another version of using rip rap for coastal protection is *gabions*. These are baskets of very heavy wire that are filled with rip rap material. They can be up to a meter on a side. These baskets may contain material that is cobble size up to boulders. The advantage that they present along the shore is not only protection from erosion but also the ability to absorb and dissipate wave energy. Their mass is large, so gabions provide a very stable protection. The only negative aspect is that the salt water will eventually cause the heavy wire to rust and fail.

The configuration of breakwaters ranges widely depending on the protection needed and the direction from which storm waves come. They may be at an angle to the shoreline, they may have a break in orientation within the structure, and they may be semi-enclosed. The latter is common for protection of boats and is quite effective (figure 4.7).

Figure 4.7
Aerial view of the harbor at Chicago, Illinois, USA, on Lake Michigan. These breakwaters are good examples of the various orientations they may have.

SHORE-NORMAL STRUCTURES

Another approach to shore protection and stabilization is to build structures that are perpendicular to the shoreline. Because longshore transport of beach sediment is a major factor in beach erosion, the main function for such structures is to interfere with the ability of longshore currents to transport sediment along the shoreline. These structures may be constructed using any of the materials mentioned above plus some other approaches. Their size, location, and specific function vary from place to place.

The groin structure is the smallest of this type of coastal structure. It is constructed so as to extend from the active beach into at least the intertidal zone. The idea is to keep beach sediment trapped in place and minimize or stop the longshore transport of sediment.

The groin is constructed with a low profile to the sediment surface that will permit sediment to build up to the desired level and then permit it to wash over the top as the longshore current moves by (figure 4.8a). If a groin is performing properly, it will have about the same amount of sediment on each side (figure 4.8b).

Figure 4.8
(a) Low groin structure that is working properly with sediment moving over its surface; and
(b) a groin field that has functioned well so that the structures are buried but still visible from the air

The size of the groin is typically related to the level of energy experienced by the beach that it is designed to protect. For example, the groins on the coast of Florida in the United States tend to be small because tidal range is small and wave energy is modest

Figure 4.9
(a) Small groins that are performing fairly well and (b) huge groin on the North Sea that is performing very well

(figure 4.9a). By contrast, the groins on the North Sea coast of the Netherlands and Germany are quite large because of the mesotidal range and the intense storm wave energy (figure 4.9b).

Groins are also made of other materials. Treated wood planks are used for small structures in the same fashion as sheet piling. Specialized groins, called *dog-bone groins*, are used in some places where small and low profile structures are preferred. These groins are made of cast concrete pieces that look like dog bones and are anchored, placed together in a zig-zag pattern across the foreshore (figure 4.10). Another groin material is the *longard tube*. These are special vinyl cloth tubes that are pumped full of sand and placed on the beach perpendicular to the shoreline in the fashion of the groin (figure 4.11). This is an inexpensive

Figure 4.10
Dog-bone groins arranged on the beach of the Florida Gulf of Mexico coast

Figure 4.11
Longard tubes that are placed to act as a groin

approach to shoreline structures, but it is susceptible to damage by both natural causes and vandalism. It is, however, easy to remove and return the beach to a natural condition.

The main problem with groins is that most do not perform in the manner for which they are intended. The typical result of installation of a groin or multiple groins is that they are overdesigned and trap too much sediment. As a result there is considerable downdrift erosion. On a global basis, there are many more groins that have performed poorly than have done the job for which they were intended.

A special type of groin is called a *terminal groin*. This is generally relatively large and is at the end of an intended beach segment, sometimes at a tidal inlet. This type of groin is designed to trap sediment and keep it from moving into another sub-environment or an inlet. In this role the groin prevents sediment from moving into a tidal inlet (figure 4.12) and the possibility of interfering with navigation in the inlet. Terminal groins tend to be effective in doing the job for which they are intended unless they are too short and the sand passes by them and into the inlet.

Figure 4.12
A terminal groin that provides a wide beach in its fillet and keeps sediment from reaching the tidal inlet

The last of the shore-normal structures is the jetty. Jetties are long structures that protect tidal inlets. Their size and configuration depends on the specific location, and they can be constructed of different types of materials. Jetty construction is like most other coastal structures: concrete, rip rap, sheet piling. The simplest configuration of jetties is two parallel structures that extend perpendicular from the shoreline (figure 4.13). They may also be curved or in an angle configuration, and each side of the inlet can be different. There are some inlets that only have a single jetty, typically on the *updrift* side of the inlet to trap sediment as it moves along the surf zone. Jetties commonly act in a similar fashion to groins in that downdrift erosion can be very severe (figure 4.14). The jetty structure is the ultimate "dam" on the "river of sand."

Figure 4.13
A tidal inlet with a pair of jetties that keep sediment from entering the inlet

Figure 4.14
Severe downdrift erosion on a tidal inlet. The terminal groin on the updrift side of the inlet has trapped the "river of sand."

In some inlet situations a bypassing system has been constructed This is basically mechanically transporting sand from the *fillet* on the updrift side of the inlet to the downdrift side in an attempt to keep the sand transport moving. This is an expensive and logistically difficult task and few have been successful.

SOFT BEACH PROTECTION

It has been the policy on many coasts of Europe to utilize various "soft" approaches to beach protection—that is, they are biodegradable or they are easily destroyed by storms. It is evident from this that such approaches to the beach erosion problem are quite temporary. The advantage is that they are environmentally "friendly" and esthetically more pleasing than seawalls, rip rap, etc. They are also relatively inexpensive.

Longard tubes or geotextile tubes are an inexpensive way to protect the toe of the dune. They are used in this fashion and also along the upper foreshore zone to directly protect the beach. As mentioned earlier, this protection works fairly well when it is not exposed to severe storms or vandalism. The tubes are not biodegradable, but they are typically not very long lasting due to physical damage. Most people find this approach to be cost effective because it is so cheap.

Vegetation in various formats can also be used to protect existing beach material and also to attract sediment that is being moved primarily by wind. The most basic of these formats is to plant vegetation (figure 4.15). Typically it is one of the common coastal

Figure 4.15 Planting grass to stabilize the backbeach and attract sand to begin to form coppice mounds

grasses that are sturdy and that require no care. This grass can stabilize the existing sand, generally on the backbeach, and attract more sand to entice dune development and growth. Trees have been planted at a few locations to accomplish the same results. One such example is near the mouth of the Gironde River in France.

Another approach to the use of vegetation is by "planting" small branches from bushes and trees in shallow ditches. These rows of vegetation extend only 30–50 cm (about 1.0–1.5 ft) above the sand substrate and are fairly effective in trapping sediment (figure 4.16). In some coastal areas on the European continent, pensioners are paid to install such protection to supplement their income.

Figure 4.16
Sticks and shrub cuttings placed in shallow ditches to attract wind-blown sand and initiate dune development on the coast of the Netherlands on the North Sea

Because of the problems with most of the hard coastal protection structures, a different approach has become very popular over the past few decades. There are various ways whereby this takes place, but the two most common are to actually put new sediment on the beach and to place materials that will attract and trap sediment on the beach. The biggest advantage of this approach is that it is esthetically more pleasing and the biggest disadvantage is that it is short-lived compared to hard structures.

BEACH NOURISHMENT

As the name implies, this approach to beach management is to place new material on the beach to replace material that has been removed by erosion. This is now the most widespread method of "fixing" an eroded beach. The biggest advantage is that the completed project looks as good, or better, than the beach looked prior to its erosion problems. It is quite compatible with the surrounding environment—no structures or "foreign" material. There are multiple disadvantages, including cost, source material, environmental impact of construction, and duration.

The cost of nourishment projects is many millions of dollars. Where does all of this money come from? The typical approach is to cost-share the expense among various levels of government from federal to local, generally in decreasing amounts. Because tax money is utilized, there are some requirements. The people's money must be used for purposes that can at least potentially benefit all people. In a few cases only local or private funds are used for nourishment.

The open beach adjacent to the shoreline is public property. This is where the nourishment material will be placed. Everyone should have access to this public property. One of the stipulations for using public money to fund these projects is that public access must be made available. This can be where a street or road ends at the beach, a pathway between houses, or via public parks. In most places some parking is made available to aid in the process. There have been small nourishment projects that were privately funded; generally no more than a few hundred meters in length. These are typically to provide a beach for a residential complex.

Environmental permits must also be obtained because a beach-nourishment project is a major engineering activity. As such, this activity can impact the beach in various ways. Very detailed construction plans must be formulated and approved as part of the permit application process. The two main variables that need to be considered are the sediment being applied to the beach and its source, and the organisms that live in this environment. Nourishment activities cannot have any important effects on beach biota. In many latitudes marine turtles are a consideration. No nourishment activities can take place during the four- to five-month nesting season. Another important factor is the benthic community at or adjacent to the *borrow site*. These communities cannot be disturbed or destroyed.

The sediment or *borrow material* used in the project needs to be as close as possible to the natural sediment on the beach in grain size, sorting, and composition. It cannot have significant mud content, which is not compatible with the beach environment. Another major problem in some low-latitude regions is the presence of living, hard-bottom communities such as reefs. As an example, the shallow marine environment just offshore of Miami, Florida, has abundant living reef communities. Miami and vicinity are also places where considerable nourishment was necessary and was carried out. Fortunately, it was possible to obtain the necessary permits for borrow material and its removal.

The volume of sediment required for these projects is huge: up to a few million cubic meters. Locating such a volume of appropriate sediment is generally very difficult. One of the limiting factors is the cost of this so-called borrow material. The material itself is typically free of cost if it comes from the underwater marine environment. Sometimes it comes from upland sources and is trucked to the project, but these are generally small projects. The distance over which it must travel from the borrow site to a major nourishment project can be several kilometers. This practice is very expensive—US$25–30 per cubic meter. Such an approach to nourishment makes a project of several hundred thousand to a few million cubic meters a huge expense.

Locating the required amount of borrow material for a large nourishment project is sometimes difficult. The two most common environments are the longshore bars that are at the outer part of the surf zone and at ebb-tidal deltas associated with tidal inlets. The flood-tidal deltas typically contain too much mud for the beach. Once located and permitted, large *suction dredges* (figure 4.17) are used to extract the sediment. The material is then pumped as a slurry of about 10% sand with water through large diameter pipes as much as a couple of kilometers to the nourishment site. In some cases the distance is too great for pumping and the material is loaded into large barges and transported to a location offshore of the site, then pumped onto the beach from there.

Figure 4.17
Large suction dredge used to extract large volumes of borrow material and pump it either directly to the construction site by pipe or onto large barges for transport and subsequent pumping to the beach

Another common method of extracting borrow material, generally for a smaller project, is using a *hopper dredge*. This is a small combination of a suction dredge, a barge, and a powerful pump that can remove the material, carry it to shallow water offshore, and then pump it onto the beach (figure 4.18). This type of dredge is also used to fill barges that then transport the borrow material to a pumping station.

Figure 4.18
Hopper dredge pumping a slurry of water and sediment directly onto the construction site

Once the borrow material is distributed to the beach site, it must then be moved and sculpted by large equipment to conform to the design for the nourished beach. The engineers always overfill the beach with more material than is needed to provide the size and shape of the completed project. This can amount to 30% in excess of the design volume. The reason for this is because the adjustment of the nourished beach to its equilibrium profile will lose sediment. Many people see this initial adjustment and think that the beach is eroding. A better term is that the beach is adjusting to environmental conditions of wave and current energy.

The completed beach is commonly stabilized by vegetation and sometimes by longard tubes. The idea is to prolong the nourishment as long as possible. Nevertheless, renourishment can be required in as short as two years. Generally it is more like five to seven years. A common reaction is that we are wasting our money spending millions of dollars only to have to do it again in a few years. All of these projects funded with tax money have been subjected to a very strict cost-benefit study prior to the funds being allocated. The amount of money that a wide, attractive beach can bring to a coastal community is typically many times the cost of the project.

There are other approaches to beach nourishment where costs can be reduced and other options are available. The most common is to use upland sources for the borrow material. Most coasts have dunes adjacent to the beach or in some cases they are older and more landward. The borrow material tends to be a little bit fine-grained compared to the beach. Dune sand tends to be finer than beach sand because it is transported and deposited by the wind instead of the water. Water has more sediment buoyancy than the atmosphere. A problem with this approach is that the dunes are generally protected for various reasons and are therefore not available for mining of their sand. Even if a permit for excavation is issued, there are other problems. The borrow material is transported by truck to the nourishment site. This requires dump trucks with about a 20 m³ capacity. Assuming a half-million cubic meter project, that means 2,500 roundtrips from the borrow site to the beach. This causes problems. First, so many very heavy trucks will damage the road on which they travel. Second, the resulting traffic congestion means that this activity is generally limited by local authorities to the late night and very early morning. Third, this type of traffic at that time of the night makes it difficult for residents along the road to sleep. The bottom line is that this approach to beach nourishment is not common.

Another somewhat different approach is to follow the above methodology but to stop after the borrow material is placed on the beach (figure 4.19). There is no grading with machine or sculpting the shape of the beach. The natural beach processes are permitted to distribute the new sediment as they would under natural conditions. This takes some time, but it is a completely natural approach and the cost is reduced considerably as compared to the more traditional methodology.

Figure 4.19 Heavy equipment moving borrow material into its proper place on the beach construction site

An even less costly and more simple nourishment approach is to remove the borrow material and transport it to a desired offshore site, commonly by hopper barge, then simply dump it at the desired depth and distance from shore. This would generally be only a few meters deep, because it is necessary for wave action to work on the sediment and carry it to the shoreline. Such a project was conducted at the southern portion of Padre Island, Texas, USA, with the sediment being placed at a depth of four meters. The borrow site was a ship channel a few kilometers away. The sediment was sucked into a hopper dredge, transported to the desired site, and dropped by opening the bottom of the dredge.

Nourishment Examples Beach nourishment projects are now being conducted throughout the world. The Atlantic Coast of the United States along with the entire Florida Peninsula has probably experienced the highest concentration of nourishment projects. Some of these have performed well, but others have not. Most of the poor performance of nourishment projects is due to the grain size of the borrow material and the wave energy, especially severe storms. Other parts of the world where nourishment has been used include Italy, Spain, the Netherlands, Denmark, China, Australia, and elsewhere. A few examples will provide some idea of how this all works.

Redington Beach, Florida, USA, provides a good picture of the before and after (figure 4.20) situation as well as the methodology of construction. This beach on the long, wave-dominated Sand Key barrier island on the west-central Florida Gulf Coast was eroding for several years, had a long vertical concrete seawall, and was in need of a major beach nourishment project. The borrow material was excavated by suction dredge from an ebb-tidal delta at Johns Pass, a nearby tidal inlet. It was pumped to the site and sculpted by machines as per the design plans. This was one of the first large nourishment projects on the Gulf Coast of

Figure 4.20a
Redington Beach
on the west-central
coast of Florida
was one of the first
of the major nourish-
ment projects on
this tourist coast.
Prior to nourishment
there was
almost no beach.

Figure 4.20b,c
Post-completion, the beach was wide and performed well. The project was completed in 1988 and the beach has been renourished multiple times since.

the Florida Peninsula and was completed in 1988 (figure 4.20). It performed well and was followed by adjacent nourishment projects at each end of the initial one. Redington Beach has been subsequently renourished as was predicted.

Miami Beach, Florida, USA, is one of the most well known beaches in the world because of the intense tourism in the area. In the 1960s and 1970s there was no functional beach in front of the many high-rise hotels where the tourists stay. One of the largest and probably the most famous beach nourishment projects took place on Miami Beach from 1977 to 1982 (figure 4.21). The borrow material was mostly carbonate sand and came from nearby offshore areas. The total cost of the project was $51 million. As expected, there is loss because this coast faces the Atlantic Ocean, although the fetch is small because of the Bahama platform. About 160,000 m³ per year are added to the area to maintain the beach that has resulted from the project. This project has been extremely successful and has remained as an excellent beach for decades.

Figure 4.21
One of the most famous, largest and most successful beach nourishment projects in North America is at Miami Beach, Florida. Shown here are (a) the pre-nourishment shoreline (1975) and (b) the post-nourishment shoreline (1978).

It is appropriate here to mention the East Coast of Florida as a site for marine turtle nesting. It is the location of more than half of the turtle nests known in the United States each year–as many as 70,000 nests of three species of marine turtles in any given year. This concentration is more than 100 per kilometer. As a comparison, the highest concentration for Texas, on the Padre Island coast, is only about 2-3 nests per kilometer. There are no data to indicate that beach nourishment has any negative effect on turtle nesting. There are restrictions on beach nourishment during the nesting season to avoid interfering with this process. In addition, hotels and other built structures are restricted from having lights shining on the beach during the nesting season because they keep the nesting turtles away.

New Jersey Coast, USA, has experienced beach erosion for decades, and beaches are one of the most important economic elements of the state both for tourism and for protection of upland structures. This state has 210 kilometers of open coast beaches In the beginning of the 1970s, 82% of the New Jersey shore was considered as critically eroding and only 9% was stable. Because of the nearly continuous development of the coast and its importance in the economy of the state, something had to be done. After studies and plans by various committees, the U.S. Army Corps of Engineers began beach nourishment in 1989 as part of an overall plan to deal with the situation. From then until 2012 this program placed close to 65 million m³ of sand on New Jersey beaches at a total cost of $600 million. Although that is a very large amount of money, it is much less than the value of the property protected.

These projects covered about 90 km of the 160 km of developed shoreline. During this time period (1989–2012) the average beach width along the entire 200 km of coast increased 30 m, although less than half of the coast was nourished. This shows how beaches adjacent to those nourished also benefit greatly from the longshore distribution of the nourishment material. A recent example from Hurricane Sandy in 2012 shows how nourished New Jersey beaches can change from a single storm (figure 4.22). This was only a category 1 hurricane, but

Figure 4.22
The coast of the State of New Jersey in the USA has been nourished for decades with mixed results. This example is from the community of Holgate.
(a) The beach before Hurricane Sandy and (b) a few days afterward in 2012.

a

b

because it came ashore at New York and New Jersey it was the second most expensive storm in recorded United States history at US$65 billion.

California, USA, beaches also require nourishment. Relatively high wave energy and sediment supply problems take a toll on beaches on this coast. Its position on a leading edge of the North American plate has produced a steep nearshore and surf zone, typically without longshore bars. The drainage systems here are very restricted in their length due to a high relief mountain system near the coast. This situation results in a dearth of sediment being delivered to the coast. In addition, the sediment that makes it to the coast is carried by longshore currents and can be captured by the head of submarine canyons that can extend to the surf zone on this coast. Once the sand enters these canyons, it is carried to deep water. All of these conditions provide coastal settings where nourishment sediment is very scarce. As a result, borrow material for these beaches must come from uplands, harbors, or directly from the mouths of rivers. This is extremely expensive and the volume of sediment available is limited.

The first nourishment of beaches on the California coast was in 1919. Most of the subsequent projects have been in the southern part of the state. Two examples from the California coast are described below: Goleta Beach and Venice Beach.

Goleta Beach is a small locally popular beach on the southern California coast near Santa Barbara. About 60,000 m³ of nourishment material were dredged from the harbor at Santa Barbara and placed on Goleta Beach in December 2003. Rip rap that protected the upland area was buried as the sand was piped in and spread along the beach (figure 4.23).

Figure 4.23
A small but popular public beach in southern California USA is at Goleta, near Santa Barbara showing (a) an erosional shoreline with rip rap and (b) the completed nourishment project.

b

Figure 4.24
Nourished Venice
beach in southern
California as it
appeared in 2011

Venice Beach is in the Los Angeles area and is one of the most popular recreational beaches on the entire West Coast of the United States, with an estimated 1.5 million visitors a year. This location was severely eroded by storms in 2004 and 2005 and then again in 2010. As a result, a nourishment project only about 0.5 km long using 25,000 m³ of sand and costing US$1 million was undertaken. It transformed the beach from being almost unusable to being beautiful (figure 4.24). This nourishment project was selected as one of the best in 2011.

North Sea Coast of Denmark nourishment has been different than most projects. This coast on the Jutland Peninsula faces the North Sea. It is not densely populated, but it is popular for tourism. This North Sea coast experiences severe winter storms with large, steep waves and wind that can reach hurricane force. As a consequence, erosion can be a problem and the coast must be managed and protected. A 110 km reach of coast has been managed since 1983, including installation of various structures and considerable nourishment of the beaches. As time passed during this management, the use of hard structures has given way to beach nourishment, which is used almost exclusively now. To date, 59,000,000 m³ of sand have been taken from the North Sea and placed on 28 kilometers of beach. In 2011 there were 1,800,000 m3 used to nourish the beaches at a cost of DKK75 million (about US$13 million). Some of the sand was placed in the shallow nearshore zone and some directly on the beach (figure 4.25).

Figure 4.25
Looking north at the central Jutland coast of Denmark showing nourishment project in the form of many truckloads of borrow material that will be distributed by the wind and high water caused by storms

The **Coast of Spain** is one of the most nourished in Europe. A big part of the Spanish economy is based on the tourism, and tourists come to Spain looking for "sun and beaches." For that, it is essential for the authorities to have good beaches. Despite this importance, there is not a general plan for beach nourishment. Instead, each spring, after the winter storms, the beaches most affected by erosion are immediately nourished so they can be ready for use by tourists at the beginning of the summer. Some of the eroded beaches are nourished each year, while others are nourished every two or three years.

A good example of beach replenishment is at La Antilla Beach in southwestern Spain in 1990. This beach has been chronically eroding over many years. It is 3,500 m long and was restored to

Figure 4.26
La Antilla Beach in southwestern Spain is chronically eroded and has been nourished multiple times. This shows the (a) pre- and (b) post-nourishment conditions.

a width of 50 m with 1,300,000 m³ of medium sand after an erosion of 50,000 m³/year (figure 4.26). The total cost of this project was US$5,333,000. A portion of the same beach needed to be nourished again in 1997. At this time, a length of 2,000 m with a width of 40 m was restored with 300,000 m³ of fine sand at a total cost of US$2,000,000. Now, 16 years later and after the strong storms of 2012 and 2013, there is a plan for a new replenishment of 1,200,000 m³ of sand, with a total budget of US$24,618,000.

Australia began nourishing beaches at the Gold Coast in southern Queensland in 1974. This is the most popular tourist area on the Australian coast and nourishment has been common. Throughout the country 130 beach locations have been nourished this century. Recent storms have devastated the beaches on the Gold Coast with both the loss of beach sand and bluff erosion (figure 4.27a). A recent study by Professor Andrew Short of Sydney University looked at the management and protection practices in this area. The community of Gold Coast is spending millions of dollars each year to pump 500,000 m³ of sand onto the beaches. Devastating storms with wind velocity in excess of 60 mph in 2009 caused major erosion and formation of bluffs in the Gold Coast area (figure 4.27a). This area was nourished with sand from various coastal and *pericoastal* environments to provide a wide and beautiful beach (figure 4.27b). The maintenance of these beaches and those throughout Australia is extremely important because they represent a major component of the tourism industry.

Figure 4.27
(a) Scarp on the beach after major erosion on the Gold Coast of Queensland, Australia, and (b) beach after nourishment

China did not begin nourishing beaches until its first project was completed in Hong Kong in 1990. Prior to that there had been considerable mining of sand from China's beaches for use in construction. Beach nourishment came along in order to support the increasing tourist use of the coast. The first mainland project was completed in 1994. Actually placing small amounts of sand on a beach was started before this in the summers, but no real nourishment projects were undertaken until 1990. After the 1990 project was completed, several projects were constructed without proper planning and engineering studies or design. Most of these were in conjunction with placement of groins and other structures to attempt to maintain the beach. This approach lasted until 2005 when larger and more sophisticated projects were constructed because of the increasing importance of tourism and the role of beaches in it (figure 4.28). These even included building an artificial sandy beach on a muddy coast. The projects ranged from about 300 m to 1.5 km in length, with the largest being 750,000 m³ of material.

A specific example is at Xiangshan-Changweijiao where erosion had been a problem since the 1950s. This location has a mean tidal range of 4 m with longshore sediment transport from NE to SW. About 800,000 m³ of medium sand was placed on 1.5 km of beach in 2007 (figure 4.28). Because of the popularity of this beach for sports such as volleyball, football, and other group sports, it was decided to widen it by about 20 m. This was accomplished in 2009 with a terminal groin added to the north end to stabilize the beach.

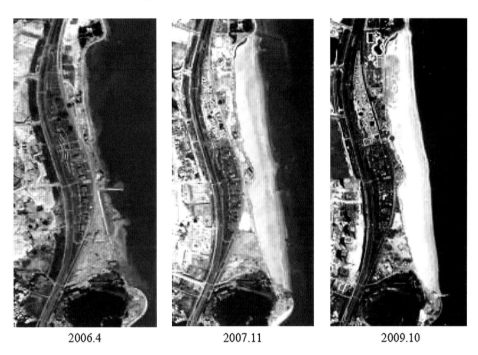

2006.4	2007.11	2009.10

Figure 4.28
Sequence of aerial images of the beach at Xiangshan-Changweijiao from the time of major erosion to the wide nourished beach

SUMMARY

People have always lived and visited the coast, particularly the beach. They have also been doing things to modify the beach; very modestly at first and very significantly more recently. All of these efforts have been aimed at trying to protect the coast and make it a better place to visit or live. As time passed and the huge crowds began to go to the beach and build next to the beach, there came the need for more and bigger approaches to protecting the shoreline and the uplands landward of it.

Hard structures were the norm beginning in the 19th century and up until a few decades ago. In some locations seawalls, groins, jetties, etc. have been shown to have negative effects on the beach and adjacent areas as well as being protective structures. These problems have led to a widespread and common approach to coastal protection in the form of "soft protection." Protection in this mode involves placing beach sediment at the shoreline. This approach is environmentally more compatible but is costly and temporary. There are also problems with available borrow material and environmental problems with withdrawal and construction. Nevertheless, it is now the standard mode of beach restoration and coastal protection. Cost-benefit analyses are required for permitting. It is not difficult to support nourishment because of the protection it provides for the upland environments, structures, and infrastructure.

5 Beautiful and Interesting Beaches of the World

There are hundreds of thousands of kilometers of beaches in the world. They range through all latitudes and longitudes from the tropics to the Antarctic. Beaches cover all tectonic and topographic settings and a tremendous range in tidal and wave conditions. None of us would be able to visit every type of beach even if we tried. I used to tell students that you can learn more about beaches from visiting a single beach location hundreds of times than you can from visiting hundreds of beaches once each. Even if that is true, it is not nearly as much fun! I hope this chapter will help you "visit" many of the interesting and beautiful beaches of the world.

BEAUTIFUL BEACHES

If you ask several people what makes a beautiful beach you will receive many answers. Some like the color of the sand; white would be the most popular. Others might like the color and/or clarity of the water. Others want lots of amenities nearby. And some want nothing but nature. I have included something for everyone.

Indiana Dunes, USA The south shore of Lake Michigan in the USA is the site of a complex of huge sand dunes. These dunes are designated a National Lakeshore by the U.S. National Park Service. There are also outstanding beaches associated with this enormous accumulation of sand. The origin of this system goes back to the glaciations of the Quaternary Period. The Great Lakes owe their origin to the glaciers with the lake basins having been "carved" out by the moving ice sheets. The glaciers also provided enormous quantities of sediment when they melted. This sediment served as the basis of the dunes and beaches along this coast. The dunes rise up to 60 m above the lake level in this area. The beaches are well-sorted sand with fine gravel in the foreshore at some locations (figure 5.1).

Figure 5.1
Beach at Indiana
Dunes Park showing
the huge dunes
on the landward side

Figure 5.2
Beach at the Indiana
Dunes National
Lakeshore where
beaches are formed
from sediment
reworked from
Quaternary glacial
sediments resulting
in some fine gravel
on the foreshore

Some of the best beaches front the largest dunes on the Indiana shore (figure 5.2). The beaches in general along the east coast of Lake Michigan display a wide range in width as lake levels fluctuate. Because there is significant variation in rainfall over many years in its drainage basin, the level of Lake Michigan has varied as well. An all-time low took place in the early 1960s, and then only 12 years later it reached near an all-time high. This increase in lake level caused beaches to erode to the point of being essentially absent at some locations. There was significant drop of lake level from the late 1970s to the end of the century and beyond. The beaches responded in kind and became wide, with steep foreshores. Sediment on these beaches is well-sorted, medium to coarse sand. The swash zone generally has some fine gravel. All of this sediment came from glacial deposits.

Destin, Florida, USA Destin is a small tourist town on the panhandle of Florida. Until the late 20th century Destin was relatively "undiscovered" by visitors. Now it is packed with them during the spring through fall months and is the winter residence of many folks from the cold northern part of the country. The reason for the interest is the combination of a great beach and beautiful water along with excellent weather.

The entire Florida Panhandle is comprised of the whitest quartz beaches in the United States (figure 5.3). The coast has essentially no fine sediment that causes the water to be filled with suspended material. This permits the water to be very clear, even in the surf zone. These beaches are generally progradational, i.e. becoming wider, with a dry backbeach and a fairly steep foreshore (figure 5.4). The beach sand is nearly pure quartz; there are very few shells to spoil its uniformity. The pure mineralogy is the result of multiple cycles of erosion, transportation, and deposition. Because of the lack of cleavage and the chemically stable nature of quartz, it has survived all of this. The beach is left with well-rounded and well-sorted quartz (figure 5.3).

Figure 5.3
Close-up photograph of pure quartz, well-rounded, well-sorted beach sand from the Florida panhandle. Bar for scale is 0.5 mm.

—— 0.5 mm ——

Figure 5.4
Florida panhandle beach and surf zone near Destin where beaches are white sand and the water is clear

Figure 5.5
Coast of California with high relief and beautiful pocket beaches

California, USA The beaches of California are among the most popular and spectacular in North America. This leading edge coast is irregular in its topography, with beautiful cliffs rising above gorgeous beaches (figure 5.5). Although the beaches shown in this figure are the most beautiful, they are generally abandoned. The popular beaches are mostly in southern California near the

Figure 5.6
Wide dry beach near Crescent City, California. Small vegetation-covered coppice mounds testify to the accretional nature of the beach.

population centers. Here surfing and other types of beach recreation are very popular. These beaches tend to be reflective because the nearshore slope is fairly steep and the waves tend to be high and long from crest to crest (figure 5.6). The tidal range in the north is up to 2.8 m; in the south it is only 1.8 m.

Tortola, British Virgin Islands The Caribbean Sea contains hundreds of islands, most of which have general characteristics in common. They have a volcanic origin and are bounded by coral reefs. This combination produces beaches that have similar characteristics. They are composed primarily of carbonate reef debris with some scattered volcanic sediment grains. Wave conditions on these beaches are generally low energy and their tidal conditions are low in the microtidal range. This location is in the path of the summer hurricanes, so storms play a role in beach conditions. The nature of volcanic-based islands is high relief with irregular shorelines. Such topography results in local *pocket beaches* between headlands. The beaches tend to be steep with beautiful, clear water (figure 5.7). They are commonly protected by a coral reef complex only hundreds of meters offshore.

Figure 5.7
Fairly wide pocket beach between volcanic headlands on the island of Tortola, British Virgin Islands. These beaches are mostly biogenic carbonate sediment with minor amounts of volcanic debris.

Spiekeroog, Germany The island of Spiekeroog on the North Sea coast of Germany is one of the sea-islands along this coast that are separated from the mainland by the Wadden Sea. These barrier islands have been occupied by people for many centuries and have been studied for several decades. All these islands are post-glacial in age, and the large volume of sediment that comprises them is composed of sediment that is ultimately from Quaternary glacial deposits, and is rather uniform medium sand. The islands here are *drumstick barriers* with considerable long-shore sediment transport from west to east (figure 5.8). This is a mixed-energy coast with a mean tidal range of nearly 3 m. There is considerable sediment accretion via lengthening on the west end of these islands, causing the tidal inlets to constrict. A tourist-dominated community exists on the wide east end of the island.

The beaches are wide, even at high tide. At low tide a significant ridge and runnel system is present during several months of each year (figure 5.9). These morphologic features can last for months as the ridge migrates onto the foreshore portion of the beach. The small cubicles in the photograph are rented or leased during the summer season and serve as a place to rest, get out of the sun,

Figure 5.8
Oblique aerial photo of the island of Spiekeroog on the North Sea coast of Germany. The arrow shows the village and the near portion is east with the direction of the sediment going to the west in the distance. The small white buildings in the foreground are tourist residences.

Figure 5.9
Wide beach and ridge and runnel system on Spiekeroog beach where numerous tourists recreate

and to keep necessities. They are all essentially the same, so the numbers identify them to their renters.

Because of the strong winter storms and the large waves that they generate, there is a seasonal nature to the beach profile. Erosion dominates the winter storm season. The large ridge and runnel systems are present in late spring through much of the summer as the sediment removed in winter makes its way back onto the beach.

Doñana National Park, Spain The beach in Doñana National Park on the southeast coast of Spain constitutes a natural system of 60 km of a pristine beach (figure 5.10) located to the east of the town of Matalascañas in the state of Andalusia. This is a highly prograding system that receives all the sand transported by the longshore currents along the coast from the city of Huelva. There is a calculated bedload transport of 300,000 m³/year. The dissipative beach has a gentle slope, with the foreshore reaching up to a width of 200 m, developing ridge and runnel systems with ridges of almost a meter high (figure 5.11). Mean tidal range

Figure 5.10
Oblique view of the pristine wide beach at the Doñana National Park on the Atlantic coast of Spain

Figure 5.11
Beach including the intertidal ridge and runnel along the coast at Doñana National Park in Spain

is near 2 m (mesotidal) and mean annual wave height is about 0.5 m. This beach is located along the front of a long spit that protects the Guadalquivir estuary marshes. In the backshore area a large foredune system is present. Landward of this foredune there are successive mobile dune chains that cover a surface of 60 km².

Australia Many people, and all Australians, believe that theirs are the most beautiful beaches in the world. That continent has by far the most kilometers of beach per capita of any place in the world. Part of that is because the entire continent has only 20 million people and beaches account for 19,000 km of beach. Another reason for their beauty is the nature of the continent. It has only a few small streams carrying fine sediment to the coast. This condition helps to keep the water clear due to the absence of suspended sediments. The sediment is pretty uniform through-out—mostly medium, well-sorted sand. Wave energy is very high during storms, but during calm conditions, swell waves with 10- to 12-second periods strike the coast. It is essentially a reflective beach because of the steep foreshore and nearshore. The beach sediment is medium to coarse sand with scattered shell debris.

A recent book by Professor Andrew Short and Brad Farmer has chosen the 101 best Australian beaches. The authors have visited all 11,761 beaches on the Australian coast, so they have a good database from which to choose those 101 examples. Choosing the best is a difficult task. This author has chosen his best as 90 Mile Beach (figure 5.12) because he has been there many times, and because it is on Professor Short's top-ten list. This is the third longest of the Australian beaches. The southeast coast of Victoria, Australia, is dominated by 90 Mile Beach, a continuous barrier island exposed to the Southern Ocean. This is a nearly pristine barrier with a steep foreshore and wide backbeach. This part of

Figure 5.12
Oblique photo of 90 Mile Beach on the Victoria coast of Australia showing part of it that is on a narrow barrier island, with the Gippsland Lakes lagoon behind it

the Australian coast can have storms that produce big waves. It can also be relatively calm at the beach with low swell waves rolling into the shore. Tidal range here is about one meter so it is a distinctly wave-dominated coast.

Victoria has some of the most beautiful beaches in Australia, typically with pure, well-sorted sand. Shells are uncommon in the beach sediment throughout this state. Ninety Mile Beach is a combination of a barrier island beach and a mainland-attached beach (figure 5.13). It has only one small inlet at Lakes Entrance on the northeast end of this trend. One of the features that make this such a nice stretch of beach is the absence of development and the lack of need for structures or nourishment. A couple of small settlements are the only development along the entire stretch of coast.

Figure 5.13
Example of 90 Mile Beach with steep, reflective beach in front of foredunes

A second Australian beach location is the Twelve Apostles National Park on the south coast of Victoria, southwest of Melbourne. It is also included in this group of examples because the overall beauty of the coast in this location is at the top of the list globally. The numerous large sea stacks are about 45–50 m high (figure 5.14). Only eight of the original twelve stacks remain after erosion has removed the rest. Limestone cliffs about 75 m high comprise much of this coast with a flat, dissipative beach. Sediment is well-sorted, medium sand that is reworked from the Tertiary strata (figure 5.15) that make up the cliffs. Wave energy from the adjacent Southern Ocean is modest except during

Figure 5.14
View of Twelve
Apostles along the
ocean road on
the southern coast of
Victoria, Australia

Figure 5.15
Beach view of two
of the stacks of
the Twelve Apostles
showing the gently
sloping sand beach

winter storms, and the stacks break up a significant amount of this energy from reaching the beach. Tides are mixed with a spring range of about 90 cm.

INTERESTING BEACHES

What makes a beach interesting? Well, some of us think that all beaches are interesting, but here we mean "special and interesting"—that is, unusual. It could be the surrounding area, the morphology and processes, the material that comprises the beach, or something of historical/cultural significance. All of these and more are covered in the following examples.

Ice-Bound Lake Michigan, USA The Great Lakes of the United States are in the mid-latitudes where winters are cold and freezing temperatures can last for some months. Lake Michigan is elongate in a north-south orientation and has well-developed beaches on both sides, although the frequent and significant changes in lake level can cause widespread erosion. These changes are dependent on changes in annual precipitation and can have a lake-level difference of 1.5–2.0 m over only a decade. The winter brings freezing conditions to this freshwater coastal zone, generally in January. Thin layers of ice, commonly a few decimeters thick, will be broken by winter storms, pushed landward by the wind to then pile up over the longshore bars (figure 5.16). This accumulation of ice forms a ridge that can rise multiple meters above water level. Generally there is a significant amount of sand incorporated into these ridges as the result of the wave action that formed them. The water there is only 1–2 m deep.

Figure 5.16
Ice at the shoreline in Lake Michigan with a ridge over the inner sandbar and open water in the distance

It is common for two of these ice ridges to form over the adjacent longshore sandbars. There may be open water beyond the ice ridges (figure 5.17), but in the event of very severe winter, ice can cover the entire lake. The ice ridges render the beach to be a zero physical energy environment during their presence. This condition is the only time where absolutely no changes are taking place on the shoreline from waves. This absence of waves generally lasts for about three months, January through March. As melting takes place in the spring, the incorporated sand becomes more

Figure 5.17
Photo of ice ridges
along the Lake
Michigan shoreline
at Indiana Dunes
National Lakeshore.
These ridges rise
several meters above
the water level.

concentrated. Eventually the ice melts to the point where spring storms will break it up and permit waves to reach the beach. It takes only a few days for the beach to revert to its pre-ice condition and look just like it did in the fall. It should be noted that this ice along the shoreline of the Great Lakes is like a temporary seawall and breakwater combined. It prevents the strong storms of the winter from doing any damage to the beach. There are situations where strong storms occur on these coasts before the ice forms, but overall the ice benefits the beach.

Big Shell, Padre Island, Texas, USA Padre Island is the longest barrier island in North America and one of the longest in the world. Most of it is designated a National Seashore by the U.S. National Park Service, so it is pristine except for scattered campers and fishermen. The beach is accessible by vehicle except that four-wheel drive is necessary for about the lower two-thirds of it. There is a dredged and jettied channel, Mansfield Pass, almost 100 km from the northern end. Beaches are generally wide and the sand is soft (figure 5.18). Like most of the Gulf Coast, the beaches are dominated by fine, terrigenous sand with various amounts of shell and shell debris. The beach is gently sloping and dissipative. Shells and shell debris become highly concentrated near the middle of the island. Well-developed foredunes are present throughout its length.

The rationale for this concentration of shelly beach (figure 5.19) is that it is at a zone where longshore sediment transport converges. This occurs because of the shape of the coast coupled with the prevailing winds from the southeast. These conditions produce a bidirectional longshore current and in turn cause sediment to move offshore at the region where the convergence occurs. Many years ago Professor Francis Shepard recognized that this was the only location along the Texas continental shelf where sediment grain size gradually decreased from the shoreline across the shelf. He interpreted this to be the result of the converging currents. The shell concentrations were left at the beach (figure 5.20) in the area of the converging currents. The section of beach is called "Big Shell" and it extends for a couple of kilometers.

Figure 5.18
Wide and soft beach on the middle of Padre Island, Texas, where four-wheeled drive vehicles are necessary for transportation

Figure 5.19
Foreshore of the beach at Big Shell on Padre Island showing the abundance of shells that comprise the beach sediment

Figure 5.20
Close-up of beach
sediment at Big
Shell showing that
the "grains" are
mostly whole bivalve
shells

Newport, Oregon, USA The Oregon coast of the United States is one of the prettiest and most interesting in the world (figure 5.21). The combination of the large trees on a cliffed coast with the wide intertidal zone provides beautiful beaches encased in

Figure 5.21
Beautiful beach on
the Oregon coast
where tides are more
than 3 m and wave
energy is high

gorgeous scenery. The spring tide range of nearly four meters produces intertidal beaches that are up to 0.5 kilometer wide but with only a fairly narrow dry beach adjacent to sandstone bluffs of Miocene sandstone. The intertidal beach is characterized by large ridge-and-runnel morphology with channels that carry rip currents (figure 5.22). This beach is well-sorted sand with

Figure 5.22
Low tide on wide, dissipative beach on the Oregon coast, USA

virtually no shell debris. The beaches on this coast display a distinct seasonal difference in appearance. During the relatively low-energy time of summer, the beach accumulates considerable sediment as shown in figure 5.23a. The high wave energy of the winter removes the beach sediment and bare rocks are common along the shoreline (figure 5.23b).

Figure 5.23
(a) Summer beach on the Oregon coast showing abundant good sand, and (b) exposed rocks during the winter indicating erosion of the summer beach with sediment being transported offshore. Line points to the same rock in each photo.

Acadia National Park, Maine, USA The coast of the State of Maine is quite irregular and is dominated by bedrock headlands mostly of granite. The geomorphology has been significantly influenced by Quaternary glaciers. There are many pocket beaches of terrigenous sand and gravel that is mostly derived from glacial drift. One of these pocket beaches is quite unusual in its sediment composition and origin (figure 5.24). It is composed largely of calcium carbonate shell debris. The shell material is

Figure 5.24
(a) Aerial view and (b) beach view, Acadia National Park in Maine, USA, that is composed completely of carbonate shell debris from three nearby shell animals including barnacles, mussels, and sea urchins

from barnacles, mussels, and sea urchins, all easily broken by wave action. These organisms are abundant just offshore of the granitic island and the shell material is transported to the beach via waves and strong tidal currents. The beach is 300 m long between the granite headlands. It has a steep, reflective profile due to high-energy storms. The tidal range is in slightly above three meters.

North Coast, Alaska, USA The north coast of Alaska has a series of barrier islands that are long and narrow, with low elevations and no vegetation (figure 5.25). These barriers are ice-fast for several months of the year—from mid-October until mid-July. This is a wave-dominated coast producing straight or sinuous and essentially shore parallel accumulations of sand and gravel (figure 5.26) that have multiple origins. The lunar tidal range is only about 20 cm, but the wind tides exceed that during open water. Even during storms the waves are rarely more than a meter high. There are pieces of tree branches scattered on some of the beaches that had to come from rivers long distances away.

Figure 5.25 Oblique aerial photo of Cross Island near Prudhoe Bay in Alaska. This photo was taken in mid-July as the ice was just breaking up in this area.

The U.S. Geological Survey has been conducting research on these barriers, along with a group from Potsdam University in Germany. Part of both of their efforts deals with global warming. The Survey personnel have found that the absence of shore ice has increased from about 80 days in 1980 to 140 days in 2010. The Potsdam group has found permafrost melting and rates of erosion increasing along this part of the Arctic coast. Both of these phenomena are important indicators of global warming.

Figure 5.26
Beach of coarse sand and gravel that dominates all of the Alaska barrier islands

Figure 5.27a
Aerial view along Chesil beach

Chesil Beach, Devonshire, England On the south coast of England there is a very famous beach that is 30 km (18 mi) long (figure 5.27a) and is composed exclusively of pebbles about 1 cm (pea size) in diameter to 5 cm (small orange) in size toward the east. The beach ridge is 150–200 m wide and up to 12 m high. This

**Figure 5.27
(b) Profile of the
gravel beach
and (c) close-up of
the pebbles that
comprise the
sediment of Chesil
beach**

steep and uniform beach (figure 5.27b) is derived from erosion of the soft Jurassic limestone cliffs near Dover (White Cliffs of Dover) that contain abundant *chert* clasts. These hard pebbles are almost perfectly rounded and very well sorted (figure 5.27c). The beach is steep, indicating high wave energy. That is puzzling because the fetch for wave development is short. A short fetch permits only small waves but they can be steep, and during storm conditions large sediment particles can be moved. Tides on Chesil Beach are semi-diurnal with a range of about 2 m.

Fishing village, Ceara, Brazil The north coast of Brazil in the state of Ceara has beaches that are home to a very interesting commercial fishing fleet. This is a coast with wide and beautiful beaches (figure 5.28). They are wide enough so that young people play football (soccer) on them. These beaches are composed of medium sand and are dominated by quartz with minor amounts of rock fragments and plagioclase feldspar. Accessory minerals are not common. Mean tidal range is about 2.5 m, just into the mesotidal range. This tidal range along with the gentle slope of the beach produces a wide intertidal beach.

Figure 5.28
Wide, gently sloping beach on the north coast of Brazil in the state of Ceara

What makes this such an interesting coastal region is the mode of commercial fishing that is conducted by hundreds of fishermen. It is unchanged from centuries ago. They use small sailboats that are only a few meters long (figure 5.29) and have no power of any kind. The hull is a flat wooden structure with a single sail and a small rack for the fisherman to lean against; there is no place to sit. Each of these boats carries a large net that is used like a purse seine to surround fish and then draw the net closed. There are only two models of these boats, one for a single fisherman and one for two fishermen. The boats are pushed through the surf in

Figure 5.29
Close-up view of one of the small, primitive boats used for fishing on the continental shelf off the north coast of Brazil

the afternoon and sailed out onto the continental shelf where the fishermen spend at least one night, sometimes two, fishing, then return in the morning with their catch. They have been making a living fishing this way for many generations.

Oahu, Hawaii, USA The Hawaiian Islands are of volcanic origin with extensive coral reefs around most of each island. The wave climate in the middle of the Pacific Ocean is one of high energy. The steep nearshore and foreshore produce a reflective beach profile. The result is one of the best surfing locations in the world, especially on the north shore of the island of Oahu (figure 5.30) where the world famous Banzai Pipeline is located. It is the site of many surfing championships, with waves exceeding 5 m in height (see Chapter 6). The sediment here, as is the case for all of the Hawaiian Islands, is a mixture of volcanic and carbonate sand. At this particular location the carbonate sand dominates because of the reefs. The sediment is well-sorted coarse sand; gravel is rare. The reason for this is the high-energy wave conditions that break up the reef material. Lunar tidal range on the island is only about 0.5 m.

Waikiki Beach on this island is one of the most famous beaches in the world. It is located in the Honolulu area on the south side of the island. It is famous because it is in numerous media advertisements, tourism brochures, movies, and other globally

Figure 5.30
Sunset Beach
on the north shore
of Oahu where
waves can be huge

distributed items of visual information. It is the place where most tourists go and where beginners are likely to do their surfing. It is also considered the romantic beach on the island.

From the point of view of this author, it is in this "interesting" category because of its widespread name recognition and familiarity to the general public. It is not really especially attractive, the water

Figure 5.31
Waikiki Beach in
Hawaii, USA,
one of the most
famous tourist
beaches in the
world. The large
hotel in the back-
ground is the
Royal Hawaiian.

is not pretty and clear, and the surfing is not especially good. The material of the beach is sand, shell, and rock—not comfortable to walk or lie down on. One of the main attractions of the beach is its location in front of the major hotels of Honolulu (figure 5.31). Like so many places in the world, Waikiki has been subject to erosion for the past few decades and has been nourished with sand from offshore and from the north side of the island.

Moorea, Tahiti The Tahitian islands, like essentially all of the Pacific islands, are volcanic based. Also like the typical Pacific island, they are bordered by coral reefs. The combination of the basaltic rock of which the islands are composed along with the coral material that is broken up by energetic Pacific waves produces beaches that tend to be a combination of black (basalt) and white (coral). One of the small islands, only 15 kilometers from the capitol island of Tahiti, is Moorea, based on a single volcano (figure 5.32). Arthur Frommer, a well-known travel author, has designated this island as the most beautiful in the world. Although visited by many tourists annually, it is rather unspoiled. One of the main attractions is the complex of thatched roof huts that are commonly visited by honeymooners (figure 5.33).

Figure 5.32
Flat, carbonate beach on the island of Moorea, Tahati. The beach sediment is derived from erosion of coral reefs that ring the island with a small amount of volcanic rock particles.

Saudi Arabia beach on the Persian Gulf The beaches of the Persian Gulf occupy an interesting location on this desert-bounded, fetch-limited water body (figure 5.34). The Gulf is typically hypersaline as compared to the open ocean, with salinity generally between 40 and 45 parts per thousand (‰) as compared to 35 in the open ocean. This relatively high salinity is because the rate of evaporation exceeds the discharge of freshwater coming in to the Gulf.

The beaches are a combination of terrigenous grains and carbonate that is of shell or coral origin. Grain size tends to average between 0.5–0.7 mm in diameter, putting it in the coarse sand category. The beach sand is well sorted except in protected areas

Figure 5.34
Oblique aerial photo
of a Persian Gulf
beach on the
Saudi Arabian coast
near Tanaqil

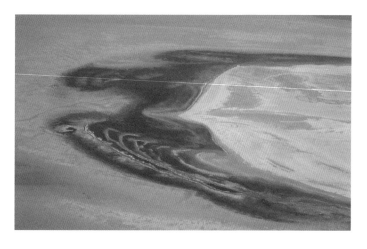

Figure 5.35
Close-up of low-tide beach near Al Jubail on the east central coast more than 10 years after the oil spill from Kuwait

where physical energy is so low that sorting and winnowing of fine sediment does not take place. Beaches are normally gently sloping and fairly wide. Average wave height is only 0.2–0.3 m on these dissipative beaches. The condition that makes these beaches so interesting is that they were covered with crude oil as the result of the Iraq invasion of Kuwait in the first Gulf War and the release of huge quantities of this oil in 1990–91. The beaches on much of this coast still have abundant oil on them (figure 5.35). The low energy conditions have prevented physical processes from reworking and distributing this oil and prevented the oil-saturated sand from being dispersed and from oxidizing.

Australia Beach Pools Beaches on much of the southeastern coast of Australia have very interesting swimming pools associated with them. Essentially on the shoreline, the communities build large, competitive swimming pools right over the beach (figure 5.36). The pools typically have lanes painted on the bottom for competition and some even have a diving area. This is a major cost for the community but it is viewed as important for two reasons: the concern about sharks in shallow water prevents many people for using the beaches in this area, and it is very difficult for anyone to swim in the nearshore area because

Figure 5.36
Large swimming pool
constructed on the
beach environment
with the natural beach
in the background on
the New South Wales
coast of Australia

of waves. The pool eliminates these problems. It should be noted that this practice is primarily from the 1950s and 1960s. Such construction is rare now.

Miazaka, Japan On Japan's southernmost island of Kyushu is an indoor beach under a removable roof. This freshwater facility is 300 m long and has a beautiful beach of crushed marble. It is located less than 2 km from the real ocean. The Ocean Dome (figure 5.37a) has been in operation for many years. It opened in 1993 at a cost of US $2 billion. It has yet to show a profit

Figure 5.37
(a) Aerial view of the
Ocean Dome near
Miazaka, Japan,
with the oceanic
coast in the back-
ground; and
(b) inside of the
dome with extensive
beaches and an
artificial Pacific
island

AMUSING PLANET

even though its capacity of 10,000 is commonly reached. The temperature is controlled and there are no bugs or dangerous animals in the water. A tropical island with an artificial erupting volcano is also present to complete the tropical beach experience (figure 5.37b).

Antarctic Beaches The beaches on the Antarctic continent are covered with ice most of the year. Even when open these beaches are exposed to very low wave energy because of the floating ice that surrounds them. All of the beach material is derived from the glacial sediment that now covers the landmass and the adjacent ocean. The sediment on these beaches ranges widely in grain size, but much of it is coarse gravel. A few of the beaches are home to a large population of penguins that use that environment as a refuge from the cold water (figure 5.38). Some beaches are gently sloping and others are steep (figure 5.39). In either case, the shoreline is quite irregular due to the absence of waves impacting on it. The shoreline is ice-free during only about two months. Because of the glacial origin of the beach sediment and the absence of waves in many places, over most of the year some beaches are composed of boulders and are not well sorted.

Figure 5.38
Ice-fast boulder
beach and
penguins on the
Antarctic coast

Figure 5.39
Steep beach on
the coast of
Greenwich Island,
South Shetland
Islands in
Antarctica.

Highly Populated Beaches Generally beaches in highly populated locations are themselves crowded . . . unless the weather is not good. This is true for all of the famous beaches of the world at places like Buenos Aires, Argentina; Fire Island, New York; Atlantic City, New Jersey, and Cannes, France. All are nice beaches, but they are crowded (figures 5.40 and 5.41). Part of the reason is that they are near high tourist areas with numerous hotels and excellent restaurants. Some beaches attract large crowds even if they are in remote places along a high-latitude coast such as in Maine, USA (figure 5.42). Back in the old days it was common for folks to go to the beach in their Sunday best to socialize (figure 5.43).

Figure 5.40
Very crowded beaches at Buenos Aires, Argentina

Figure 5.41
Huge crowd at surfing contest, Huntington Beach, California

Figure 5.42
Huge crowd on the beach at a beach on the coast of Maine, USA

Figure 5.43
Beach crowd in their Sunday best at Atlantic City, New Jersey, USA,
in 1915

Not all crowded beaches are crowded with humans, because many species enjoy the beach experience. The nature of these beach occupants differs from geographic region to region. One of the most unusual is an extensive beach along the Antarctic coast where penguins enjoy walking on the wide, gently sloping beach (figure 5.44). In the Galapagos Islands, the beach is a good napping place for sea lions (figure 5.45).

Figure 5.44
A large number of penguins strolling along Antarctic beaches

Figure 5.45
A group of sea lions having a nap on a beach in the Galapagos

SUMMARY

In this chapter we have looked at a wide range of beaches distributed over a wide range of places on Earth's surface. The composition covers a broad spectrum and so does the sediment particle size. Waves and weather in general produce a wide range of scales and shapes to beaches everywhere. Regardless of where one is located or the specific nature of the beach, a visit is always a fun experience. It is more fun if the weather and water are nice, but even a good beach on a bad day and a bad beach on a good day are experiences we enjoy.

6 Human Activities on the Beach

Once humans occupied the coast, and specifically the beach environment, a significant influence on the natural system was imposed. The earliest people settled on the coast for two primary reasons: transportation and food. Both were essential to sustain their communities. Eventually these important activities have given way to others, some for survival and protection, others for recreation. They include major conflicts, sports, important works of art, movies, and more. All of these activities require some knowledge of beaches—their morphodynamics, composition, and performance through time.

BEACHES IN WARS

The Mediterranean, Red, and Aegean Seas have been the site of conflicts for millennia. The northern coasts of Europe have also been major locations of invasions from the Celts, Vikings, and other early civilizations, as well as wars in the 20th century. Because water was the main avenue of transportation, the beach was the destination of many invasions. Sometimes a beach was even the site of battles between adjacent countries that shared a mainland boundary. More recently, many important battles in World War I and World War II involved beach landings of combatants.

The Greek navy commonly used the beach as a landing location as early as the 5th century BC. The Greeks preferred to stay close to the land and maneuver into position for battles at sea or for moving onto land to engage the enemy. The Romans were less adept at naval operations at this time. Ancient Egyptians used a navy primarily for transportation of goods and personnel rather than direct conflict. They did use ships to protect the Nile Delta, the shoreline of which extended across almost the entire northern margin of the country.

The ships of ancient history were small, shallow-draft vessels that moved with many men rowing and/or sails. Soldiers could be transported to shallow water just offshore of the beach from where they could walk to shore and move landward to meet the enemy or march landward to confront them.

Some well-planned and organized invasions of coastal areas took place in the 16th century. Examples include the Turks invading the island of Malta in 1565 and Spanish marines invading the Azores in 1583. The Spanish marines continued their invasions with good success in the 18th century at Sardinia in 1717 and Sicily in 1732. These military activities expanded to North America, with the British landing at Canada in 1759 and the Continental marines at Nassau, Bahamas, in 1776. All of these invasions were based on infantry soldiers being off-loaded from small landing vessels to the beach. Not all beaches were suited to this type of activity. The island of Malta has steep narrow beaches and high relief landward of them. By contrast Nassau in the Bahamas is very low relief, with shallow nearshore and wide, gently sloping beaches. During the American Civil War in the early 1860s, the Union conducted coastal invasions on each of the Confederate coastal states.

WORLD WAR I

We have good information on the beach invasions and other conflict activities on the coast during World War I. Most of the activity was in the Mediterranean and Aegean Seas, with some on the north coast of Europe. One of the best documented of the beach landings in World War I was on the Gallipoli Peninsula on the Turkish coast. One of the main transport ships that participated in the landing was the *River Clyde,* built in Glasgow, Scotland, in 1905 and requisitioned for the Royal Navy in 1915. The ship was able to move close to the shore and deploy troops through staircases into the shallow, low-energy surf zone (figure 6.1). The painting shows the troops moving down the gangways across the shallow water and onto the beach.

Numerous diaries and photographs from soldiers and journalists have found their way into newspapers and magazines in the Western world. Most of this information was taken from *The Guardian* under the name of Sergeant D. Moriarty. Gallipoli was not a particularly good place for a beach landing because the beach was narrow and steep and the terrain going inland was also quite steep (figure 6.2). The landing troops were predomi-

Figure 6.1
Painting by Charles Dixon of the *River Clyde* troop ship unloading troops onto the beach at Gallipoli on April 15, 1915

Figure 6.2
Steep beach where troops landed at Gallipoli, a very difficult place to establish a beachhead

nantly Australians and New Zealanders and were inexperienced at this type of invasion. The enemy was dug in and killed 17 while wounding 200. Fighting continued until mid-July when the Allied troops retreated from the peninsula at the end of a long and brutal siege. This battle eventually led to ANZAC Day (Australia and New Zealand Army Corps), an important military holiday for Australia and New Zealand, celebrating this invasion and the soldiers who gave their lives.

There was an important German invasion on the islands that controlled access to the coast of Latvia in the Gulf of Riga on the Baltic

Sea. This took place on 11 October 1917. It was a very successful campaign for the Germans, who took over the islands in a month and forced 20,000 troops to abandon them. These Baltic islands have beaches that are conducive to landing troops (figure 6.3): relatively gentle nearshore and beach slopes, low wave energy, and accommodating landward terrain facilitated coastal invasions. Tidal range is so small it was not even considered in the landing.

Figure 6.3
The Gulf of Riga beaches where a major invasion on the coast of Latvia took place: (a) the natural beach as it probably appeared at the invasion, and (b) the beach now with a health spa and folks enjoying the beach.

WORLD WAR II

Because World War II took place in two quite different arenas—the Pacific and European theaters—the respective beaches in each played somewhat different but important roles. In Europe the beaches are extensive and connected to a large landmass while the Pacific is dominated by small islands. Tidal range on the European coast is multiple meters and in the Pacific it is quite small. The differences in the specific environments are numerous, but the military approach was similar in both situations.

PACIFIC

Pacific islands are mostly small and are covered by volcanoes, some extinct, some dormant, and some active. The nature of the beach is similar regardless of the activity of the volcanoes. Volcanic sediment along with some reef debris comprises the beach materials. The particles can range from sand-size to boulders of both origins. Tidal range on these islands is typically small, with spring ranges from about 0.5 to 1.2 m. The steep nearshore and high wave energy cause the beaches to be narrow and steep. Both of these factors enter into the planning of an invasion. The absence of significant tides eliminates the need to have major concerns about tidal stage during the landing. The steep slope of the beaches coupled with the small tidal range means that the beach is fairly narrow. The nearshore bottom surface is also relatively steep, permitting waves to reach very near the shoreline.

These parameters mean that the landing crafts that carry personnel can reach the beach and unload essentially at the shoreline. It also means that wave action can be a major limiting factor. As a result, weather predictions were very important to any invasion plans. There are other important factors to such invasions, but the beach and beach processes must be considered.

Iwo Jima This island is probably the most recognized location of World War II in the Pacific. It is a small, volcano-based island northwest of the Mariana Island chain. The landing of troops on the island is a classic example of the conditions described above. The steep, reflective beach, dark volcanic sand, and small waves along the shore provided good conditions for this famous landing (figure 6.4). This battle lasted for a few weeks, from February 19 to March 26, 1944. Each side lost thousands of men, much more than the entire Middle East conflict of the early 21st century. The result was the capture of the entire island and the erection of the American flag as depicted in many illustrations and statues. The beach was a major factor in permitting the landing and establishment of positions of the United States Armed Forces.

Figure 6.4
Landing of Marines
on Iwo Jima showing
the steep beaches
composed of dark
volcanic material:
(a) large vessels right
against the shoreline
and (b) a submarine
at the shoreline
indicating deep water
very near the beach

ATLANTIC

Although there were multiple landings on the Mediterranean coast, the most well known and most important were on the northern coast of Europe. The Normandy invasion was the one that was critical to the eventual outcome of the war in Europe. On June 6, 1944, the invasion began at 6:30 A.M. This became the largest coastal invasion of all time. It involved several countries and over 150,000 Allied combatants in the overall activity (figure 6.5).

In the days preceding the invasion there was concern about the weather. Finally on June 5 the weather cleared to the point that it was acceptable to proceed. The stage of the tide was a consideration. The mean spring tide along this coast is 9-11 m—extremely

Figure 6.5
The landing of the Normandy invasion of Allied troops on the north coast of France was the largest of World War II. Thousands of troops came ashore on the beaches at 6:30 in the morning of June 6, 1944. The photo above shows a spectrum of invading troops, landing crafts, transport vessels, etc.

large—and is also semi-diurnal. Such a large tidal range requires significant planning for an invasion of this magnitude. In addition, the tidal currents in the English Channel are very strong, especially at a spring tide. To add another problem to the situation, the Germans had placed obstacles in the shallow coastal waters to inhibit the landing craft and the personnel from moving onto the beach. This led to the need to wait until low tide for the landing. At low tide during a spring condition, most of the obstacles would be exposed and could be avoided, therefore making the landing less difficult.

The choice was made to take advantage of the low spring tide conditions for the landing. Going onshore at high tide would have permitted the landing craft with troops to come close to the likely battleground. On the other hand, coming at low tide allowed the landing crafts (figure 6.6) to avoid obstacles placed in the inter-tidal zone by Germans.

A thorough study of the beach and coastal processes took place over about a month prior to the date of the invasion. It was found

Figure 6.6
View from open
landing craft showing
the infantry troops
moving into the surf
zone with the beach
in the background

that the lower intertidal beach was gently sloping and dissipative with small waves under non-storm conditions. The intertidal beach was almost 300 m wide. The upper portion of the beach, including the entire foreshore and backbeach, were dominated by well-sorted pebble-size gravel (figure 6.7). This part of the beach reached 2.5 ms high and about 14 ms wide, and was reflective. Bluffs rose up to 50 m above sea level at one end of the beach.

Figure 6.7
Photo showing Omaha Beach (a) as it appears now as a wide gently sloping beach with the upper part gravel and the lower part well-sorted sand; and (b) close-up showing the well-sorted nature of the very well-rounded pebbles that are about 5 cm in diameter

Omaha Beach was the most fortified and was the most difficult on which to establish a beachhead. Only two of the sixteen tanks made it to the shore. Of the 50,000 men, 5,000 were lost. Eventually the beachhead was stabilized, but the cost of the first day was severe.

The Normandy coast of France is now a very popular tourist location. Tours of the various sites and locations are visited by many people, including some of the veterans who landed there under the worst of circumstances (figure 6.8).

Figure 6.8
World War II veterans walking on one of the Normandy beaches

SPORTS ON THE BEACH

The beach and adjacent shallow marine environment is a great place for sports of various kinds. The combination of good weather, sandy substrate, and water provide an excellent venue for outdoor activities, both of an individual and team nature.

SURFING

When one thinks of surfing there are a few places that come to mind immediately: Australia, Hawaii, California, and South Africa are at the top of the list. Each of these coasts has conditions that are excellent for this sport. Generally one needs a long fetch, long period waves, and an appropriate nearshore profile. Although nobody surfs on the beach itself, good surfing places generally have great beaches.

Figure 6.9
Wave breaking over a surfer on the Banzai Pipeline on the north side of the island of Oahu in Hawaii

The Banzai Pipeline on the north side of the island of Oahu in Hawaii is probably the most famous surfing location in the world. Many international contests are held there because the waves are both well formed and huge. It is not unusual for the steep wave front to exceed 5 m in height as the wave breaks over the innermost of three reefs (figure 6.9). The beach here is almost

pure carbonate originating at the reefs and is very steep with a reflective profile. The steep beach creates a stadium-like setting for folks watching the surfers (figure 6.10).

Much of the Australian coast is good for surfing. The most popular are the Gold Coast of Queensland and the Sydney area on the Pacific coast, but the best waves are probably on the southwest coast in the Indian Ocean, south of Perth. The area at Margaret River is where many international surfing contests are held because the waves are the best (figure 6.11). This is not a single location but a series of great wave breaks spread over more than 100 km of coast. The beach is excellent throughout this area. Because it is not near a population center, the remote nature of Margaret River is also an attraction.

Figure 6.10 Steep, amphitheater-like beach, composed of carbonate reef debris where people watch the surfers at the Banzai Pipeline

One of the most beautiful of the Margaret River beaches is at Injidup. This is a pristine beach with no amenities except for a small parking lot and a stairway to the beach. The water can be quite calm (figure 6.12), but when the swell rolls in over the breaks, the surfers come. The beach is wide, with white sand and clear water.

Figure 6.11
Large and outstanding surfing wave breaking at Margaret River, Western Australia

Figure 6.12
Injidup Beach on the coast of South Africa

Most people know surfing in South Africa from the 1966 movie *Endless Summer* in which surfing buddies traveled the world looking for the perfect surf. They found it on the Atlantic coast of South Africa. The beaches are wide, composed of quartz-rich sand, and the water is clear (figure 6.13). The surf is large and perfect (figure 6.14), attracting numerous international contests.

Figure 6.13
Jeffrey Bay, South Africa, probably the best surfing locality in the world

Figure 6.14
Great wave and surfer on the coast of South Africa west of Cape Town

VOLLEYBALL

Beach volleyball is widely popular. It is even an Olympic sport. The nature of the beach lends itself well to this sport as long as the beach is wide enough and composed of sand and lacking large rocks and shells. The sport began in California in 1922 and was played by six-man teams, much like the indoor version. The first two-man games began in 1930, also in California. Beach volleyball comes in two basic forms. One is just a fun pick-up game played by whoever is present at a beach party (figure 6.15). The most organized and the Olympic-level type is with two-person teams, male or female (figure 6.16). This version requires very talented and physically fit participants (figure 6.17).

Figure 6.15
Pick-up volleyball game at the beach in conjunction with a picnic/party

Figure 6.16
German women's beach volleyball team at the 2012 London Olympic Games

Figure 6.17
Professional female volleyball player going after the ball

The original version of beach volleyball is like the indoor version, played by six people. There are outdoor variations of the six-person game, but they are not a major aspect of the sport. It is mostly played by people of all ages who just want to have some semi-organized fun on the beach. The organized, Olympic version for women's teams is quite popular in the United States, Brazil, and Germany. The strong men's teams are from the United States, Russia, and Italy. The beach version is very popular at all levels and now is also played indoors as well, with real sand in an artificial setting. It is probably the most widely played beach sport.

RUNNING

The beach is an excellent place to run for exercise and for getting one's body into great physical condition (figure 6.18). Two basic approaches are taken depending on the objective of the activity. If distance and cardiovascular performance are the reason for the run, the best choice is a smooth, hard-packed beach such as those on which vehicles travel. On the other hand, running on a soft beach is very strenuous and is good for improving one's stamina. Most people who jog or run for exercise consider it to be an important but boring activity. Doing it on the beach makes it much easier to tolerate. If a person really wants to get into excellent physical condition, an excellent method is to run up the dunes behind the beach. The combination of soft sand and the steep slope is about the most strenuous running there is.

Figure 6.18
Woman jogging on the beach, a common and fun exercise

FISHING

Surf fishing is a really popular sport wherever there are beaches and adjacent surf. For practical purposes, that is every coast where beaches exist. This can be a year-around sport unless the beach becomes ice-fast in high latitudes. Water temperature is not a deterrent due to chest waders. The ability to drive on the beach facilitates this activity because it permits the fishermen to access remote beaches and to carry all the gear that they need, including camping equipment, food, etc. (figure 6.19). Typically large and sturdy poles are used for surf fishing. Commonly each fisherman maintains more than one pole (figure 6.20) and the poles are held by a holder pushed deep into the soft sand.

The best beach and surf conditions for fishing are where the nearshore slope is gentle and longshore bars are present. A heavy weight on the fishing line to stabilize the bait is required in these locations to compensate for the waves. Fishing is best in the troughs between the sandbars. The basic approach is to wade as far as possible into the surf and then cast the weight and bait well out into the surf. Because of the heavy weight it is sometimes difficult to tell if you have a bite.

Figure 6.19
Surf fishermen with their poles at the steep beach on the North Carolina Outer Banks, USA

Figure 6.20
Sometimes the
fishermen abandon
their poles for
lunch or a nap.

AUTO RACING

Daytona Beach, Florida, USA, has great historic significance for
the sport of auto racing. First of all, this is one of the few beaches
in Florida on which driving is easily done. The beach is wide,
gently sloping, and generally smooth except after a bad storm.
This was recognized in the 1930s and races with various vehicles were held, initially on the straightaway on the beach. In the
early 1950s an oval track was conceived by combining the beach
with State Highway 1A which parallels the beach about a block
inland. This made it possible to have fairly long races using a
conventional oval track (figures 6.21a and b). These beach races

Figure 6.21
The races on the
beach at Daytona
Beach, Florida,
gave rise to
NASCAR racing
in the United
States: (a) from
1952, and
(b) a more modern
version.

were the first of the stock car races and gave rise to NASCAR, the most popular spectator sport in the United States. The last race held on the beach was in 1958, the year before the current Daytona Speedway opened.

CAMPING

One of the best venues for camping of most any kind is on the beach. This activity is generally somewhere accessible by car, coach, or boat. Vehicles (though sometimes only four-wheel vehicles) are permitted on many beaches throughout the world. Typically boat access is not directly on the beach because of wave action. The most common approach for boats overnight is from the back of a barrier island, the more narrow the better. Beach camping can range from throwing a sleeping bag on the sand to very upscale coaches. (Some people can stay for weeks without having to leave for provisions.) Local, state, and federal parks offer camping next to the beach in the United States and other countries.

Beach camping presents some difficulties. The easiest approach is with a self-contained coach with a generator, bathroom, full kitchen, and sun shade. The only problem is the sand and salt spray. There is commonly a breeze over the beach. Sand gets into almost everything and can make things miserable. The good thing about the breeze is that it keeps mosquitoes down. Other beach camping runs the gamut from camper units on a pick-up truck to simple tents (figure 6.22). A real outdoorsperson will simply put a sleeping bag on the sand, climb in, and try to sleep. Amenities may be absent under the above circumstances but the avid beachgoer does not worry about that as long as the beach is a nice one and the surf is good.

Figure 6.22
Camps for fisherman set up on Padre Island, Texas, where surf fishing is popular. They range from
(a) tents to (b) RVs.

MINING THE BEACH

Sand is a very important commodity, especially for construction, as a major component of concrete. In some countries or regions of a country it is scarce, just as it is for beach nourishment. Other beach materials are also economically important. These minerals are in only a percent or two of the sediment and are used in paint, abrasives, and other products. This beach mining is not limited to developing countries; it can occur in many places. Nowadays mining beaches for sand is basically forbidden because the beach environment is such a valuable resource for protecting upland areas and as a tourist destination.

Mining beach sand for construction purposes does not discriminate between terrigenous and carbonate beaches; both work well. Such mining ranges from small, one-man operations to larger-scale activities using large machines that produce a significant volume of material (figures 6.23a and b). There are some places where mining for specific minerals is still permitted because the volume of material that is removed is small and the beach can be returned to its original and natural state. The most common example of such mining is removing what are called heavy minerals. These include a range of mineral species that are both chemically and physically resistant to destruction. They comprise only 1–3% of the beach sand and can be removed easily because of their high specific gravity—generally at least 2.85 gm/cc. Included are garnet, zircon, rutile, and other mineral species that are generally used in various industrial manufacturing.

Figure 6.23a
Man shoveling
sand from a beach
in Puerto Rico
onto a wagon

Figure 6.23b
Front-end loader
and dump truck
mining a beach
for construction
purposes

b

ARTISTS ON THE BEACH

Everyone considers the beach to be a great place to spend time. In various ways all beaches are beautiful. It can be the water seaward with breaking waves, dunes that have tall grasses on the landward side, or in some places the wetlands that are on the landward side of beaches and dunes. All of these environments, as well as the folks who come to spend time there, are of interest to artists. People have been painting and photographing beach and adjacent environments for many years; in the case of painting, for centuries. Sometimes it is simply the scenery that captures the attention of the artist. Other times it might be people, animals, or boats.

Setting up an easel on the sand and painting the scenery is both relaxing and satisfying. The painted scene can include most anything, including the water itself. A painting by the Dutch artist Ary Pleysier (1809-1879) is a beautiful example combining people having picnics on the beach with sailboats beyond (figure 6.24). It shows a wide and gently sloping beach with a dissipative profile. A contrasting beach scene was painted by an Italian, Antonio Leto (1844-1913). It was painted on the coast of Capri in 1907 and shows a developed shoreline area surrounded by buildings (figure 6.25). The beach is narrow and steep, showing a reflective profile although no significant waves are illustrated. Tides are less than 0.30 m at Capri. This location is protected from storms so beach erosion is not severe.

Figure 6.24 (top)
Ancient ships landing on a beach in the painting *Beach View With Boats* by Ary Pleysier

Figure 6.25 (bottom)
1907 painting by Antonio Leto showing the developed coast with little beach, Capri, Italy

A watercolor of the coast after a hurricane was depicted by the famous American artist Winslow Homer (1836-1910). The painting shows a native Bahamian lying on the narrow, steep beach next to his wrecked skiff after being washed onshore by the storm. In the background the waves are still rough as the storm slackens. Evidence of its fury is shown in the form of the combination of the broken boat, the rough water, and the stormy sky (figure 6.26). These Bahamas islands are composed entirely of calcium carbonate sediment that is a mixture of shell debris

Figure 6.26
Painting by Winslow Homer showing a young man who apparently washed up on shore in a storm

and chemical precipitates. Beaches are white to pink, generally wide, dissipative, and prograding. Tidal range throughout the island complex is about 30 cm.

The painting shown in figure 6.27 is *Children by the Beach* by Louis Michel Eilshemius (1864-1941). He was a prolific American artist whose work ranged from landscapes to portraits. This painting shows three children with their small sailboat on the beach. Another small sailboat is in the background on this rather flat beach. The painting was done in 1909 at an unknown location.

Figure 6.27
Painting from 1909
by Louis Eilshemius
showing young boys
on the beach with
their small sailboats

Figure 6.28
Sculpture on the
beach by Gerry
Stecca of Miami
made of clothespins

The last example of beach art is also one of the most interesting. It is by the contemporary artist Gerry Stecca from Miami, Florida. He works in a single medium: clothespins. The sculpture shown here is a human figure sitting on a wide and beautiful beach, hands on knees (figure 6.28). The setting is probably a part of the wide and nourished Miami Beach. This is a gentle profile with a dissipative beach and small waves in the background.

These few examples have shown a rather wide spectrum of art subjects from different places and subjects with the beach in common. Next time you see someone sitting in front of an easel on the beach, go up and have a chat. You will learn something!

BEACHES IN MOVIES

Movie locations include virtually all places on the planet and throughout the universe. Some very famous and endearing movies had well-known beach scenes. The subjects range widely. *From Here to Eternity* was one of the first movies (1953) to have erotic love scenes, as shown here (figure 6.29). It shows Burt Lancaster and Deborah Kerr in each other's arms while the surf washes past them on the foreshore of a Hawaiian beach.

Figure 6.29
One of the most famous of all movie scenes took place on the beach: the embrace by Burt Lancaster and Deborah Kerr in *From Here to Eternity* in 1953

Dr. No (1962) was the first of the James Bond movies starring Sean Connery. This one included some beach scenes from Jamaica (figure 6.30). The beach here is low energy with a low tidal range. The Bond Girl is Ursula Andress.

Figure 6.30
Sean Connery as
James Bond strolls
along the beach
with Ursula Andress
from the first Bond
movie, *Dr. No,*
in 1962.

One of the most famous beach scenes of all movies is from *Chariots of Fire* (1981) showing runners from the United Kingdom training for the Olympics by running on the beach (figure 6.31). These beaches on the British Isles are subjected to high tidal ranges, so at low tide one runs on a hard packed exposed beach surface and at high tide over soft and dry sand.

Figure 6.31
The scene of the runners on the beach from the 1981 movie,
Chariots of Fire

Figure 6.32
The gorgeous beach at Koh Phi Phi, Thailand, from the 2000 movie
The Beach starring Leonardo DiCaprio.

An extremely beautiful beach appeared in the movie *The Beach* (2000) starring Leonardo DiCaprio. It was filmed on the coast of Thailand at Koh Phi Phi. The isolated nature of the location is one of the things that make it beautiful (figure 6.32).

SUMMARY

The beach is home to a wide variety of activities, some fun and beautiful and others horrible. Some are voluntary and recreational and others are mandatory and involve very intense conflict. The bottom line is the beach is a really interesting place for human activity. There are no age restrictions—everyone can enjoy the experience.

Selected Readings

Bird, E.C.F. *Coastal Geomorphology.* New York:
John Wiley and Sons, 2008.

Carter, R.W.G.; C.D. Woodroofe; and O. van de Plassche.
Coastal Evolution. Cambridge, MA: Cambridge University
Press, 1997.

Davis, R. A. *Beaches of the Gulf Coast.* College Station, TX:
Texas A&M University Press, 2014.

Davis, R. A. (ed.). *Coastal Sedimentary Environments,*
2nd ed. Heidelberg: Springer-Verlag, 1985.

Davis, R. A. (ed.). *Geology of Barrier Island Systems.*
Heidelberg, Ger: Springer-Verlag, 1994.

Davis, R. A., and D.F. FitzGerald. *Beaches and Coasts.*
Oxford, UK: Blackwell, 2003.

Fox, W.T. *At the Sea's Edge.* Englewood Cliffs, NJ:
Prentice-Hall, 1983.

Haslett, S.K. *Coastal Systems.* New York: Routledge, 2009.

Neal, W.J.; O.H. Pilkey; and J.T. Kelley. *Atlantic Coast Beaches.*
Missoula, MT: Mountain Press, 2007.

Pilkey, O.H.; W.J. Neal; J.T. Kelley; and J.A.C. Cooper.
The World's Beaches. Berkeley, CA: University of California
Press, 2011.

Short, A.D. *Beach and Shoreface Morphodynamics.*
Chichester, UK: John Wiley and Sons, 1999.

Figure Credits

All images not otherwise designated are by the author.

Glossary

backbeach That part of the beach that is dry under normal conditions; between the swash and the dunes.

barrier island An accumulation of sand at the coast that is formed primarily by waves with some help from tides. They typically have beaches along their entire extent.

bathymetry Measurement of the depth of water in oceans, seas, or lakes.

beach An accumulation of sediment along the shoreline that is subjected to waves.

beach nourishment Adding sand to a beach in order to increase its width and improve the protection of the upland environment.

bedload The sediment being transported near the bottom of the water column in a current.

bimodal sediment A sediment that is a mixture of two populations each of which has a statistical mode, therefore it has a bimodal texture.

borrow material The sediment that is taken from one place and used to nourish the beach; generally seaward of the beach.

borrow site The location from which the beach nourishment material is taken.

breakwater A hard structure placed seaward of the beach that is designed to shelter an area from wave attach; it may be protecting the beach or can be protection of moored boats from waves.

chert A very fine grained variety of quartz, sometimes called flint.

cleavage Planes of weakness in the crystal structure that split easily.

collision coast A coast that is located where two crustal plates are coming together.

continental shelf The extension of the continental mass beyond the shoreline into the ocean. It is wide on a trailing edge and narrow on a collision edge.

coppice mounds Small accumulations of sand on the backbeach typically anchored by vegetation; an incipient sand dune.

delta A large accumulation at the mouth of a river or stream where it empties into a basin such as a lake, sea, or ocean.

dissipative beach A gently sloping beach and nearshore where energy is reduced as the wave moves across the nearshore.

dog-bone groin A groin constructed of interlocking sections of reinforced concrete pieces that look like dog bones.

downdrift erosion Erosion of the beach on the down-current side of the longshore sediment transport.

drumstick barriers Barrier islands that have one wide end and one narrow end, and look somewhat like the drumstick of a chicken.

estuary A type of coastal bay that received both fresh water from the river(s) that empty into it and sea water from tides.

fetch The distance over water that the wind blows.

fillet The accumulation of beach sediment on the updrift side of a jetty or other shore-normal structure.

fluvial Refers to anything associated with rivers.

foredunes The first row of dunes that is landward of the beach.

gabions Cube-shaped, heavy wire baskets filled with rip-rap material and used to protect the shoreline.

glacier A huge accumulations of ice and snow that covers a large area and that lasts for many years.

glacial drift All of the sediment that was deposited by glaciers regardless of grain size or composition.

groin A shore-normal structure that is placed at the beach and extends into the nearshore.

hardness A relative property of a mineral grain based on a scale of 10 (diamond) to 1 (talc 1).

heavy minerals A group of minerals that have a specific gravity in excess of 2.85 gm/cc and are chemically stable so they persist through time. Examples are garnet, rutile, magnetite, and staurolite.

hopper dredge A relatively small dredge that sucks sediment up into a large hopper then transports the borrow material to a desired location and opens the hopper to dispense the sediment to the sea floor. It can also pump the sediment on to the beach.

hurricane A cyclonic weather system where the wind velocity is a minimum of 74 mph.

isostatic rebound The vertical change in land surface elevation as the result of the release of the huge ice mass when glaciers melt.

jetty Hard structure placed along the sides of inlets at the open water side. Jetties are designed to protect and stabilize the mouth of the tidal inlet in order to maintain a channel for vessel traffic.

lithosphere Refers to rocks of the earth, from the Greek derivative "lithos."

longard tube A plastic sleeve that is filled with sand and used to protect the shore area from erosion or to stabilize the shore area.

longshore current A current that develops in the surf zone as the result of wave refraction. It may be rapid and can carry large volumes of sand along the beach.

longshore sandbars Sandbars in the surf zone that parallel the shoreline and that typically cause waves to break over them.

macrotidal Coast where the tidal range is more than 4 m.

mean grain size This is the average grain size for sediment and is measured using phi units (ϕ).

mediterranean A marine water body that is smaller than an ocean such as the Gulf of Mexico or the Mediterranean Sea.

mesotidal Coast where the tidal range is between 2 and 4 m.

microtidal Coast where the tidal range is less than 2 m.

morphodynamics The series of cause and effect changes that take place in modern sediment environments such as the beach. Basically it is a change through time.

mud Any sediment that ranges between 4 microns and 62.5 microns in diameter. Not common but present on some beaches.

neap tide The minimal tidal range that develops during the first and third quarters of the lunar cycle.

nearshore The zone immediately seaward of low tide that is typically characterized by longshore sandbars and troughs. It commonly coincides with the surf zone.

nekton Animals that can swim and overcome currents.

ooids Spherical sand grains composed of thin concentric layers of calcium carbonate.

paleogeographic maps Maps that show the geography of ancient times.

pericoastal Around or in the vicinity of the coast as in perimeter.

placers Sediment grains of high density minerals that act as a lag deposit during erosional conditions. Gold is a good example because it is 14 times as heavy as water.

plate tectonics The slow movement of crustal plates around the earth surface, both verticaland horizontal.

Pleistocene Epoch Most of recent period in geologic time, Quaternary, during which glaciers were abundant. It began about 2.6 million years ago and ended 10,000 years ago with the beginning of the Holocene.

pocket beach A small beach that is located between adjacent rocky headlands in a "pocket."

plunging waves Waves that gradually steepen and then break instantaneously.

Quaternary Period The last period of the geologic time scale that began 2.6 million years ago and continues today.

reflective beach A steep beach and nearshore that permits much wave energy to reach the shore where a considerable amount of the energy is reflected.

refraction The bending of wave crests as they move into shallow water and approach the shoreline.

relative sea level The change in the position of the sea surface in comparison to the position of the earth's surface.

revetment A structure to prevent erosion of property.

ridge and runnel An intertidal bar (ridge) and trough (runnel) that commonly develops after a storm and is a temporary feature of a beach profile.

rip current A seaward-moving current in the surf zone as setup water moves through saddles in the longshore sandbars.

rip rap Rocks of various size and composition that are used to protect the shore area.

river delta A large accumulation at the mouth of a stream where it empties into a basin such as a lake, sea, or ocean. It requires a place to come to rest such as a continental shelf.

roundness The smoothness of the edges of a sediment grain; a circle would be perfectly rounded.

salient An accumulation of sediment on the shoreline in the lee of a shore-parallel structure.

sand Sediment particles that range between 2.00 and 0.625 mm in grain size.

sea-level rise The slow increase in sea level as water is added to oceans through the melting of glaciers.

seawall A hard structure at the shoreline designed to protect the coast from erosion.

setdown A decrease in water level near the shoreline due to the friction of offshore wind blowing over the water.

setup The temporary increase in water level at the shoreline due to onshore wind and resulting waves.

sorting This is a measure of the uniformity of the grain size of the sediment and is the statistical standard deviation (second statistical moment). It can best be determined by using the grain sizes as phi units (ϕ).

sphericity The approach to equidimentional of a sediment grain; a sphere would be perfectly spherical.

spilling waves The type of breaking waves that break over some distance and a few seconds; not instantaneous.

spring tide The maximum tidal range that occurs during the new and full moon of the lunar cycle.

storm beach profile The beach profile after a storm where erosion has occurred and the foreshore is generally relatively steep.

storm surge The vertical increase in water level caused by strong onshore wind especially during a hurricane. A part of this water level increase is also caused by the low atmospheric pressure in the storm.

storm tide The same as a storm surge.

subsidence The sinking of land due to mass and compaction.

suction dredge A large dredge that removes sediment through a combination of rotation of a large bit and suction of the sediment up to be transferred into a barge or pumped on shore.

surf zone The band of breaking waves along the beach. The width changes with the size and energy of the waves.

surging waves Those waves that are the last to break as they move onto the foreshore zone.

terrigenous Derived from land. Refers to all sediment that came from bedrock on land through various means of erosion.

terminal groin A generally large groin at the end of a beach segment, sometimes at a tidal inlet.

tide-dominated Coasts that owe most of their morphology to tidal processes. The depositional elements tend to be shore-normal in orientation.

tide gauge An instrument placed on a stable foundation in a coastal environment that measures and records the fluctuation of water level at that location.

tieback A steel rod or cable that is anchored to the seawall at one end and behind the wall to a deadman buried in the ground.

trailing edge coast A coast that develops on the margin where crustal plates are moving apart.

tropical storm A cyclonic storm where the wind exceeds 39 mph.

typhoon The eastern hemisphere equivalent of a hurricane.

undertow A seaward-moving current that is the adjustment to setup with water flowing along the bottom.

updrift The side of the inlet or any other location to which the current if flowing.

washover channel A channel excavated by the storm surge forcing water over a beach, generally on a barrier island.

washover fan A fan-shaped accumulation of sediment that is deposited landward of the beach by storm conditions.

waves Regular surface disturbance of the water surface that progresses across the surface.

wave-dominated These are coasts or coastal environments who owe their primary morphology is due to wave action. The main features tend to be elongate and shore-parallel.

wave refraction The bending of a wave crest as it approaches the shoreline at angle and the speed changes from place to place on the crest.

wind tide The increase or decrease in water level caused by sustained wind; generally onshore (increase) or offshore (decrease).

Index

M

macrotidal, 12, 43, 44
magnetite, 34, 35, 36
Malta, 136
Margaret River, Australia, 145, 146
Mariana Islands, 139
marine turtles, 83, 90
Massachusetts, USA, 29
mean grain size, 26, 28
Mediterranean, 7, 23, 64, 135, 136, 140
medium sand, 45, 97, 99, 102, 106, 109, 110, 122
mesotidal, 12, 41, 45, 48, 77, 108, 122
Miami Beach, Florida, USA, 89-90, 158
Miazaka, Japan, 128
microtidal, 12, 48, 105,
migrating ridge, 20, 21
Miocene Epoch, 51, 52, 116
Mississippi Delta, USA, 63, 65
Moorea, Tahiti, 125-126
morphodynamics, 15-23, 135
mud, 6, 25, 26, 39, 44, 61, 65, 84
mussels, 118

N

NASCAR, 151, 152
National Seashore, 113
neap tide, 13
nearshore, 13, 16, 17, 18, 6, 47, 69, 70, 92, 95, 105, 109,
     123, 127 129, 136, 138, 139, 144, 150
nearshore bathymetry, 13
Netherlands, 37, 77, 82, 88
New Jersey coast, USA, 91-93,
New Zealand, 34, 35, 47, 137
Newton's Law, 12
Niger Delta, 65
Nile Delta, 64
90-mile Beach, 109
Normandy, 140, 141, 143
North Sea, 37, 48, 77, 82, 95, 106, 107

Here are some other books from Pineapple Press on related topics.

For a complete catalog, write to
Pineapple Press, P.O. Box 3889, Sarasota, Florida
34230-3889

or call (1-800)746-3275.
Or visit our website at www.pineapplepress.com.

Florida's Living Beaches by Blair and Dawn Witherington.
Detailed accounts of over 800 species, with color photos for each,
found on Florida's sandy beaches. Covers plants, animals, minerals,
and manmade objects.

Florida's Seashells by Blair and Dawn Witherington.
Accounts, maps, and color photos for over 250 species of mollusk
shells found on Florida's beaches

Living Beaches of Georgia and the Carolinas by
 Blair and Dawn Witherington.
Lists over 850 items found along 600 miles of Atlantic coastline.
Color photos highlight birds, turtles, fish, mammals,
flowers, and much more.

Seashells of Georgia and the Carolinas by
Blair and Dawn
Witherington. Color photos of hundreds of the shells you'll find
on the beaches of Georgia and the Carolinas, including details
about the features, habitats, and diet of each shell's inhabitant.

Our Sea Turtles by Blair and Dawn Witherington.
A comprehensive narrative of every aspect of sea turtles' lives, from
egg laying to human rescue efforts. Includes stunning color photos,
maps, illustrations, and charts that reflect sea turtles' unique contri-
butions to our environment. Meticulously researched.

Best Beach Games by Barry Coleman.
Discover 75 simple, engaging games you can play on the shore
with your kids. Most of the games require nothing more than items
normally found on the beach.

Just Yesterday on the Outer Banks, Second Edition,
by Bruce Roberts and David Stick.
Celebrates the history and uniqueness of North Carolina's Outer
Banks with photos and text that feature shipwrecks, lighthouses,
fishermen, beaches, and even picket fences. Historian David Stick's
gentle prose accompanies images by renowned photographer
Bruce Roberts.

Shipwrecks, Disasters & Rescues of the Graveyard of the Atlantic and Cape Fear, Second Edition, by Norma Elizabeth and Bruce Roberts. Covering 1750 to 1942, this slim volume highlights the most famous shipwrecks and sea disasters that occurred off the coast of North Carolina. Filled with color and black-and-white historical illustrations and contemporary photographs, this is a treasure trove of facts and details about these wrecks and rescues.

Shipwrecks of Florida by Steven Singer. The most comprehensive listing now available of over 2,100 shipwrecks from the 16th century to the present. Extensive appendices offer a wealth of information for divers and researchers.

Bansemer's Book of the Southern Shores by Roger Bansemer. An artist's journal describing in words and paintings the natural beauty of the coasts—from the sponge divers of Tarpon Springs to the marshlands of coastal Georgia.

Guardians of the Lights by Elinor DeWire. Stories of the fortitude and heroism of the men and women of the U.S. Lighthouse Service, who kept vital shipping lanes safe from 1716 until early in the 20th century.

The Lightkeepers' Menagerie by Elinor DeWire. Stories of animals that have lived at lighthouses, including bell-ringing dogs, swimming cats, parrots, deer, bears, foxes, horses, mules, goats, and cows. This thick volume is loaded with vintage photos and endearing stories of animal companions and includes an 8-page color section.

The Lighthouses of Greece by Elinor DeWire and Dolores Reyes-Pergioudakis. Lavishly illustrated and carefully researched, this full-color book covers over 100 lighthouses, \most still guiding ships around the Greek Islands.

Lighthouse Families, Second Edition, by Bruce Roberts and Cheryl Shelton-Roberts. What was it like to live and work at a lighthouse during the heyday of shipping and fishing? Filled with first-person accounts and loads of family photos, this is a record of the memories and stories of America's lighthouse keepers.